RAISING DADDY

Diane Harvey

Raising Daddy

Copyright © 2022 by Diane Harvey

ISBN 979-8-9864660-0-2

Published by Sandstone Publishing
Interior design by Jera Publishing
Cover Illustration by Gilbert M. Young

Dedication

Lakeisha, Demario, Johnny, Cheryl, Brandon, Dorian
and
Caregivers

Contents

My Soul Looks Back and Wonders

How I Got Over
Negro Spiritual

ALL I COULD THINK of was that I didn't want to die! How could I be sure that I would live long enough to complete the goals that I had put on hold for the past nine years? Voice acting, writing, and hosting a radio show topped my list of dream jobs! What I saw happen to close friends who were caregivers, taught me that I only had to live for *one more year* to have my shot!

My eyes were focused on finishing the first-year-post-caregiving race. Three dear friends did not cross that finish line. Gale was in her mid-50s when she died suddenly, four months after her mother. Cathy in her late-50s, kept cancer a secret until she lost her battle with it seven months after her father passed. Richard was 56 when he died of a heart attack, nine months after his caregiving journey. I was 59 when Daddy died. I had to get out of my 50s!

I lived in fear of dying for a year after Daddy died. The starting pistol was fired on August 19, 2014. From that moment on, I was horrified that the slightest headache, cough, rash, or hangnail was a symptom of something fatal. I braved having knee surgery two months after Daddy's death because my chronic limp had become noticeable and the pain unbearable! I didn't see that as terminal since my knee had troubled me for years, so I classified that as a preexisting condition! I never considered surgery earlier because I couldn't take care of Daddy while recuperating from the procedure.

Taking care of someone you love, who can no longer take care of themselves, is a job that sneaks upon you like a thief in the night. You are completely unprepared for the abrupt changes it brings. There is no way for you to know how many twists and turns this rollercoaster ride will have. The world is spinning so fast that you can't even formulate questions to ask for help. You simply run around like a chicken with its head cut off trying to figure it out. You *never* figure it out. However, you keep moving! And it's through that constant movement that you find a way…*your way*!

I am writing this book to share how I found *my way.* As I was navigating around in that dark room, I hit a lot of bumps and got many bruises… physical and emotional. The healing from those bruises continued years after Daddy died. In the Gene Hackman movie *I Never Sang for My Father,* Hackman's character said, "Death ends a life. But it does not end a relationship…" I wholeheartedly agree! Daddy's death was the beginning of my making sense of and learning to value our father-daughter-caregiver relationship!

Caregiving is confronting death on a daily basis through someone you love. You know what lies at the end of the journey, no matter its length, is *death.* You cross your fingers and hope that the death isn't yours! After taking care of Daddy for almost 10 years, he died the day after his 94th birthday. I knew that if I could survive until August 19, 2015, I would be fine.

I don't remember many details of my life during the first year after Daddy died. Probably because the healing from my knee surgery was quite an uphill climb. I still found time to agonize over the occasional stress-induced headache, cough, rash, and hangnail. I didn't update my living will, so I must have believed that I would cross the year mark.

On August 19, 2015, I celebrated! I survived a year after Daddy's passing and a few months later I made it to my 60th birthday!

Caregiving is like fingerprints...*all different.* My story is just that, *my unique experience.* There are no right answers. There's only what works and what works *better.* However, if I could write a prescription for taking care of yourself while caregiving for others it would include high dosages of patience, permission to cry and scream as needed, acceptance that your life was disrupted, and approval to be angry as hell! Heavy on the *angry as hell*! That's where the venting helps release your pain. And for the record, you deeply love the people you care for. The challenges of taking care of them doesn't erase that, it *allows* it.

The Pre-Empt

*"When we least expect it, life sets us on a challenge to
test our courage and willingness to change…"*
Paul Coelho, Brazilian lyricist and novelist

A STROKE AND HEART attack flipped the roles between
my dad and me. To call this a transformation would be an understatement…it was an *evolution* and a *revolution*! We would have
to sculpt out a new *normal* as our reversed roles reconfigured our
relationship forever!

I knew something was dreadfully wrong when out of the ordi-
nary, I received a phone call from my father on a Wednesday! Usually
he called Saturday morning at 8:00…*every* Saturday morning at 8:00.
I never bothered setting an alarm because his call woke me. We
chatted exactly 15 minutes about the weather, how my kids were
doing in school, and if I needed money. He lived in Gary, Indiana and
I live in Atlanta, Georgia. My mother started this weekend ritual,
but instead of 15 minutes we talked for well over an hour! When
Mama died suddenly in 1990 from an internal hemorrhage, Daddy
picked up the gauntlet and continued the Saturday calls, which he
reduced to his normal 15 minutes! To hear from him on a weekday
was not only an anomaly, but also a reason to panic!

In the middle of a monthly staff meeting my phone rang, and on the screen appeared "BJ". That was the name his fraternity brother William Roach had given him when I was in high school. My maiden name is Jenkins. One Saturday Mr. Roach called our house and asked to speak to *Jenkins.* Recognizing this baritone voice was that of an adult male, I knew it wasn't a call for my brother or me, so I jokingly asked, "Which one?" Mr. Roach laughed and told me that he wanted to speak to the big one, *Big Jenkins.* We shortened it to *BJ* and that was his nickname forever.

I leaped from my seat and ran outside to answer the call. "BJ are you okay!" I shouted, because he was hard of hearing. I detected a subtlety of fear in his voice as he responded, "I have a headache." My heart was pounding like a drum by then! Given his high tolerance for pain, if he complained of a headache, his head must have been ready to explode! "Call your doctor," I instructed. From my medical social work experience, I knew that headaches could be a sign of high blood pressure, which could lead to something serious like a heart attack or stroke. Daddy assured me that he would be fine.

The next day at work another call came. Same complaint. The following day another call with yet another headache. I surmised that these calls were not simply headache alerts, but SOS signals! He was 83, hypertensive, and diabetic. True to his Leo zodiac sign, he possessed the qualities of a lion. He was fearless, independent, and leader of the pack. It was hard for him to ask for help, especially from me. I was his youngest child and it was *his* job to take care of me. Up until now, people came to him for help. Mr. Jesse Jenkins, a gentle giant with his hearty grin, thick black-rimmed glasses, and cigar was the fixer of problems at home and work.

It was over 40 years ago in the 1960s that Daddy worked as a social worker at his alma mater, Roosevelt High School. We lived several blocks away from it. In those days it could take up to 30 minutes to do what I called *cook coffee.* Daddy would go to his office to start percolating the coffee, come back home to eat breakfast, then return to his office. A slew of coffee-club drinkers who paid 15 cents a week to enjoy their morning drink of Folgers, served in a white Styrofoam cup, awaited him. Only now he had retired and didn't have regular contacts with the teachers, counselors, administrators, secretaries, cafeteria ladies, or custodians that once comprised his work world. He did, however, have regular contact with *me*...every Saturday morning!

The fact that he called me made it my responsibility to fix things as he had done many times in my life. I remember when I was in the 4th grade and wanted to be a Girl Scout. The local troop wasn't accepting new girls. My dad saw me struggle to fight back tears when I told him that I didn't get in. A few days later, I received a call from the scout leader inviting me to the next meeting! I remained in scouting through high school! The second biggest event of my life was the debutante cotillion. It was the social affair of the year for high school senior girls! Since childhood I had dreamed of being a debutante strolling out on center stage with Daddy...me in a beautiful white formal gown and him in a white tuxedo. Mama would be seated in the *Debutante Mothers Section* of the balcony in a gorgeous new dress! The icing on the cake was that my picture would be featured in the local newspaper! Shortly after submitting my application to the sponsors of the 1974 cotillion, I was rejected. It was the Girl Scouts all over again! Daddy recognized those familiar tears as a sign of my aching heart. Once more he sprang into action! Without ever knowing what he did, I was invited to participate in the cotillion! Daddy fixed it because he couldn't bear to see me hurting. Even though Daddy wasn't crying, I couldn't bear to know that he was alone and physically hurting.

It was January 2005, and the Martin Luther King three-day holiday weekend was approaching. I had to go to Gary to check on Daddy, but several obstacles threatened my plan. I didn't have any money, my car needed servicing, and I would have to board my dogs. Now *I* was the one getting a severe headache. I cried. Not a simple boo-hoo-hoo whimper, but an OH-GOD-WHAT-AM-I GOING-TO-DO outburst! My ringing phone caught me mid-sniffle and I rushed to answer it thinking it was Daddy. It was my lifelong best friend Debbye. Within seconds I was pouring out my heart to her in between sniffles, nose wiping, and gasps. She told me to come get her brand new Land Rover! Next, I called my best friend Michelle who, after the sniffling-nose-wiping-gasping routine, brought me her Shell gas card. Things were looking up! Moments after hanging up from Michelle, my sister-friend Gloria called. At the end of my saga, she went to the ATM and withdrew $300 for me. My final conversation was with my son Mario, who was attending nearby Tuskegee University. He generously offered to come home to puppy-sit Sydney and Gracie. Wow! I had completely forgotten about them! All obstacles removed, I grabbed a handful of my favorite CDs to play on my excursion and off I went.

Reflections

- *Life has interruptions.*

- *Friends step up during crises. Be thankful for them!*

The Move

"Toto, I have a feeling we're not in Kansas anymore."
Frank Baum, *Wizard of Oz*

THE MUSIC OF THE Temptations and Sam Cooke kept me bouncing and upbeat on my 11-hour journey home. I left Atlanta at 5:00 Saturday morning and arrived in Gary that evening. I was overwhelmed with joy as I entered my neighborhood! Pleasant memories of my childhood returned such as learning to ride a bike, building a snowman, and squeezing in the last game of hide-and-seek as the streetlights flickered, were vivid. Beaming with glee I smiled at our small red brick house as I pulled into the driveway. Climbing out of the car I whispered, "Hi house, I'm home!" Stretching my legs and shaking off my travel fatigue, I dug through my purse for the house keys and headed to the front door. What I saw upon entering the living room instantly wiped the smile off my face! My father, who was usually up and dressed by 6:00 in the morning, was still wearing his red plaid wool robe and blue striped cotton pajamas! His thick, short gray hair hadn't been combed, his smudged eyeglasses had slipped down to the edge of his nose, and he looked weak.

"BJ are you okay?" I asked with alarm as I looked at him slumped in our vintage emerald wingback chair.

"What time is it?" he asked.

"It's dinnertime. Have you eaten yet?"

"I don't know," he responded slowly.

My mind began racing out of control! *Something was wrong! Daddy was a diabetic. Had he taken his medicine? Had he completely lost track of time? How long had he been off of his normal routine? Why wasn't he dressed?* Within minutes I knew I had to bring him back to Atlanta! "Put on some clothes so we can go eat," I said hoping to jump start him. It worked! Immediately his disposition changed and he was coming back to life!

While Daddy happily got dressed, I grappled with how I would approach the difficult subject of him coming home with me for a few weeks. Daddy hated leaving his house for more than a week. I needed him to visit a doctor in Atlanta to determine the cause of his headaches. When we arrived at the restaurant, Daddy guzzled down a plate of baked chicken, collard greens, cornbread, and mashed potatoes as I rehearsed the conversation in my head. *I would say, "BJ, I want you to come home with me." He would shout, "No!" My comeback would be, "Yes you are, because you can't keep calling me at work every day complaining of a headache." He would then look over those smudgy glasses and say, "You don't tell me what to do!"* That's as far as I got before the waitress brought a slice of sweet potato pie. As much as Daddy enjoyed eating food, dessert was the best part of his meal. When he plunged his fork into the pie, I knew it was time to strike! My voice quivered as I geared up for a fight, "BJ, I want you to come home with me for a while to see a doctor about your headaches. I can't take care of you long distance." Without hesitation, he cheerily agreed.

I shook my head in disbelief! *Now what? I wasn't expecting him to respond favorably and certainly not so quickly! Where was he going to sleep? Did he have a three-week supply of medicine? How could I retrieve his medical records? I didn't even know who his doctors were!* In a flash I went from feeling nervous about a fight to feeling overwhelmed with a barrage of questions with no easy answers! Daddy was obviously feeling much better now and was all smiles and laughter. Conversely, I was trying to maintain a smile while falling apart inside!

Returning from the restaurant to Daddy's house, I remembered my doctor-friend who would occasionally make house calls to Daddy for me. Since this was a weekend, getting everything I needed would require an inside job, thus I called him. Fortunately he was still in the office and agreed to stop by. The only payment he requested was beer. Daddy kept plenty of it in the fridge! While my friend tossed back two cans, Daddy called a couple of buddies to tell them that he was going to Atlanta. He was so exuberant that you would have thought he was en route to his favorite vacation spot, Las Vegas! Two neighbors came by to wish him well and discuss arrangements to oversee the house. My doctor-friend made plans to email the medical records that he could not access immediately and wrote prescription refills for all of Daddy's medications. Packing a few of his clothes, meds, insulin needles, and extra pair of eyeglasses was all I could do before getting rest for the long journey back to Atlanta.

Monday morning I woke up ahead of Daddy to carefully map out our breakfast, lunch, and dinner stops...critical parts of any trip for a diabetic. Before leaving he would eat a bowl of Corn Flakes, sort of a *pre-breakfast,* to coat his stomach to take his insulin shot and 15 different pills. I had planned meal breaks in cities where I also needed to stop for gas. We would stopover in Nashville for supper and our final gas refill. My sister Sandra lived there so I planned for her to join us. Daddy loved food, which helped him to maintain his 268-pound frame! Eating on the road and dining with Sandra would be highlights of the trip! By the time Daddy arose, he was rested and ready to go. In his absence his neighbor George was going to pick up the mail. Neighbor John promised to keep an eye on the house and shovel the driveway if it snowed. I gathered Daddy, his luggage, all his medical necessities, and *his* favorite CD's, and this time off *we* went.

Reflections

- *The only preparation you can have for the unknown is determination.*

Entering a New World

MERGING ONTO THE I-65 ramp heading toward Indianapolis we were not only leaving Gary, but also everything that was familiar to Daddy. We were driving away from his neighbors, former coworkers, Bridge club, gambling boat, church, his home for the past 45 years, and most importantly…his independence! At this point, we weren't sure if he'd return. More than 10 hours later as we crossed the Georgia State Line, we stepped over a threshold into a new world. The last time Daddy was in the South, it was a society where Jim Crow Laws strictly enforced racial segregation. He was a soldier in the Army then. As we were growing up, he often shared stories of his time at Fort Benning in Columbus, Georgia. He spoke of segregated restrooms, and entertainment spots where white soldiers could go, but not the blacks. Daddy had not been in the South since 1940-something and didn't know what to expect. I was re-entering a world that only days ago I lived in as a liberated woman. I had been divorced for more than 20 years and had successfully raised two children. I survived making last-minute science projects, attending parent-teacher conferences, participating in field trips, and shopping for proms…along with other emotional and financial stresses. I was now looking forward to a future of hanging with friends, dating with the prospect of marriage again, traveling, and attending formal galas... along with low stress and financial freedom. But here came Daddy.

Mind you my dad's view of his life didn't include him spending it with me either! Other than the week-long visits with each other in July and at Christmas, he was accustomed to preparing his own microwave meals and going about his life. It certainly did not include me controlling his every move, whereabouts, careabouts and what-nots! So began the process of coexisting.

I had no idea how this cohabitation would look. I was 21 years old the last time I lived at home with my parents. My mother, brother, and grandmother were key players in our family structure then. Daddy and I had our ups and downs, but always landed on our feet. Our love unified us and in times of discord, interventions from the key players were welcomed. I remember one incident as if it were yesterday. I was 15 and Daddy was teaching me how to drive. We did fine until we got to the parallel parking part. He yelled at me for getting too close to the car behind me and I started crying. Then he shouted at me to stop crying and park the car. Now I was angry, so I screamed back, "I'm trying to do it!" I obviously had a moment of temporary insanity because raising my voice at either parent never ended well! I guess Daddy knew he had pushed me too far, because he didn't say anything else. When we got home, I couldn't wait to tell my mother about my horrible driving experience! I was overly dramatic! Complete with flailing arms and exaggerated gestures, I told Mama that Daddy could not give me another parking lesson... *EVER*! She ignored me and continued cooking as if thinking, *Y'all work that out!*

Finding no support there, I called my grandmother to report Daddy's offensive behavior. She assured me that she would punish him. That was more like it! I could always count on Grandma for an emotional assist! She had proven to be a reliable ally after I learned that she was Daddy's mom...a discovery I made when I was five. We all lived in the same apartment building and I hung out with Grandma every day. She told endless stories about Daddy as a youngster. I asked her how she knew so much about him and she said, "I'm his mother." *What! Why hadn't someone told me this? I just thought her name was Grandma.* At that moment I didn't realize that we were related, but I knew that mothers could punish their kids! That's all I needed to know. Whenever Daddy mistreated me by fussing at or denying me any request, I threatened to tell his mother. She promised that she would spank him. Though I never saw her actually do it, I trusted that she took care of things. This was our pact for life! I don't know why I bothered going to my mother in the first place about this parking incident. That was his sweetheart and partner. She was always going to take his side! Neither Daddy nor I could hold a grudge for long. Within a few days, all was forgiven and we were back to the parallel parking lessons.

Six months before Daddy's arrival in Atlanta, I had just purchased a new ranch-style house. I gave him the master bedroom because it was the largest and as a show of respect. He also needed the bathroom inside the master to spread out his medications. The main bedroom with a king-size bed also made him feel like king-of-the-castle! And since he was only planning to stay for a few weeks until we could get his headaches under control, I could sleep on a twin bed in the smaller bedroom temporarily.

When he walked in the house, I escorted him to the bedroom to unpack his clothes. He looked around and asked, "Am I going to sleep in here?" I smiled but never answered. By this time Sydney and Gracie were following Daddy and sniffing him like a new chew toy! Daddy enjoyed the attention and patted them on their heads. I was amazed that we had completed a day-long road trip without one headache complaint! *Was he really sick or just lonely?* The answer came the next day.

I was worn out when I returned to my job on Tuesday. I made it through the day! But on the drive home, my cell phone rang. It was Daddy calling to report a headache. I sped home and took him to the nearest emergency room. The doctor gave him painkillers and sent him home. He felt better Wednesday, so I went to work. My day was cut short at 2:00 in the afternoon, when Daddy called about his pain. I left early and we made a second trip to the emergency room only to be administered painkillers and sent home again. Feeling frustrated, I called my friend Cynthia whose elderly mother was a regular patient at Emory Hospital. I told her about our unsuccessful trips to the emergency room. I needed help on what to do because I couldn't leave work daily! Cynthia advised that if I had to take him to the emergency room again, take him to Emory instead of the hospital near my house. She explained that if Emory admitted him, he could bypass the waiting list for admission to their Wesley Woods geriatric facility. The next emergency room trip happened two days later.

Friday started out great! Daddy was feeling fine when I left home and I had made it the full eight hours at work without a call from him. That peace was short-lived. When I got home, Daddy was sitting on the side of the bed holding his head down. I dropped my purse and ran to his side to see what was wrong! "My head is hurting again. I didn't want to bother you at work, but it's really bad!" He said. I told him not to worry that we would go to the emergency room again, but at a *different* hospital. He sighed as if hoping that this emergency room visit would have better results than the last two. I fed the dogs and took them outside to potty before heading to Emory. The weather was changing. The temperature dropped and snow was expected. Since I didn't know how long we would be away, I grabbed some cookies and crackers for Daddy on the way out of the house. Diabetics always need snacks in case of insulin level drops.

There was a crowd when we arrived at Emory's emergency room. I thought since Daddy was the oldest person there, he would get preferential treatment. He wasn't having a heart attack or bleeding openly, so we had to wait in line. After signing in and completing the required check-in procedure, the triage nurse met with us to assess the reason for our visit. She wrote some notes on a clipboard before taking his blood pressure and other vital signs. The nurse wrapped a nametag around Daddy's wrist and walked us to a tiny pod with a thin curtain that separated us from the other patients. Daddy hopped on the gurney and pulled back the curtain so that he could see and enjoy the hoopla going on in the emergency room. We saw a cast of characters while waiting for the doctor. A man with a broken arm screamed for over an hour. He obviously didn't think the medical staff realized that his squawking meant pain, because occasionally he would toss in the words, "It hurts! It hurts! I'm in pain!" Finally a nurse gave him a shot of *something* and he settled down. Daddy looked at me and calmly asked, "I wonder how he broke his arm?" Next, a gunshot wound victim was wheeled by us. Since he was bleeding, he got moved to the head of the line. Again Daddy faced me and questioned, "I wonder how he got shot in the leg?" A nurse came in several times to take Daddy's blood pressure. It was high. He complained of a headache, so the nurse gave him a pain pill and told us to give it about 30 minutes to work. Daddy was hungry and asked for a sandwich. The nurse told him to wait for the pain medicine to kick in before eating. Thirty minutes later, his blood pressure slightly lower and headache a bit diminished, the nurse ordered a turkey sandwich and a Diet Coke for him. He rarely chewed food thoroughly and gobbled his snack in minutes! By the time the emergency room doctor came to Daddy's pod, his blood pressure was back on the rise. This time higher than before!

Thankfully I had Daddy's medical records with me. I told the doctor about a previous minor heart attack, the frequent headaches which made me bring him from Gary to Atlanta, and the two emergency room visits to another hospital days earlier. He ordered an electro-cardiogram and other tests. Hours later we were still awaiting results and Daddy's blood pressure continued rising. It was after midnight and the doctors had changed shifts. The incoming physician was a lady who planned to release him if his pressure came down, so she ordered more pills. By now the snow was falling hard and many car accidents had occurred. I begged the doctor to admit him, at least for the night. It was snowing so badly that if he had a headache the next day, I might not be able to drive through inclement weather to bring him back. During my pleading with her, Daddy drifted to sleep. When he awakened, he asked, "Am I ready to go home?"

"Not yet Daddy."

"What's wrong with me?" He queried.

"What makes you think that anything is wrong?" I asked trying to sound comforting.

"I see it on your face," he snapped.

He read me accurately! I was terrified. *Why wouldn't his blood pressure stabilize? He had suffered a heart attack several years earlier and had a stent in his heart. If his pressure did not come down, he would have a stroke! He was too old to survive that! Surely he did not come here to die.* The doctor came back with good news and some *almost* good news. She decided to admit him for observation. He would be going to Wesley Woods, which was about a mile away. I vigorously shook her hand while graciously thanking her! Then came the *almost* good part. She said that due to all the car accidents, the paramedics were tied up and she didn't know when a rig would be available to transport him. I asked if I could drive him there. I saw the look of uncertainly on the doctor's face about my plan. She quickly scanned the emergency room and saw that it was filling up with accident victims, so she reluctantly agreed to let me take him. The nurses gathered his test results, medical records, and situated him in a wheelchair. I dashed to the parking lot to get my car and drove it up to the emergency room entrance. Snow was sticking to the ground and ice was forming. I trusted that my sturdy 1990 Volvo 240DL could get us through the storm safely. I had been to Wesley Woods before so I knew where it was, but I was about to learn that I didn't know that it had two entrances. I also didn't know that the rear one wasn't open after midnight.

Icy roads turned a 5-minute drive into a 30-minute crawl. When I drove into the empty parking lot, I wondered why there were only a few lights on inside. Then it hit me, *this was the wrong entrance!* I was at the back and I didn't know how to get to the front. I saw a doorbell and figured if I buzzed it someone would come to direct me. I left the motor running to keep Daddy warm and told him to stay in the car as I walked to the building. I rang the bell, but no one answered. I banged hard on the door and still no answer! Panicking, I ran back toward the car and saw Daddy opening his door and stepping out. "NO DADDY DON'T GET OUT OF THE CAR! WE'RE AT THE WRONG DOOR!" I screamed! Before I could reach him, he had fallen. I couldn't determine if he had slipped on the ice or passed out. Either way he was lying flat on his back and was unconscious inhaling the fumes from the car's exhaust pipe! *What just happened! Did he hit his head on the curb when he fell? I didn't see blood, so that was a good sign.* I ran back to the door this time pounding like crazy and yelling, "SOMEBODY HELP!"

This experience was turning into a scene from a scary movie. It was a dark snowy night and I was standing alone in freezing weather! Daddy lie motionless on the ground, possibly even dead and I didn't know what to do. I was trembling with fear, but didn't cry! Realizing that tears wouldn't help anyway, I fast-forwarded to prayer! Here's the thing, I was between religions. After 15 years as a Methodist, I had started studying Buddhism and was only in my infancy stage of practice. I hadn't learned much about it and didn't know what Buddhists do in crises. I chanted *Nam Myo Renge Kyo*, then immediately defaulted to my Christian roots, "GOD HELP ME!" One or both worked because I calmed down enough to regain my focus! I shimmied out of my coat and tossed it over Daddy's face to keep the snow off his glasses. Next, I ran around to the driver's side of the car, reached in and turned off the ignition. Noticing my cell phone on the dashboard, I grabbed it and frantically punched 9-1-1. After explaining my urgent situation, the operator calmly asked, "Where are you?"

"I'm at Wesley Woods at Emory! I think I'm in the back!" I shouted.

"Is your father breathing ma'am?"

I wasn't sure, but remembering what I learned from medical TV dramas, I yanked Daddy's glasses off his face and placed them under his nose. When I saw the foggy motion on the lens, I shouted, "Yes! Yes! He's alive!" The operator assured me that help was on the way and the sound of sirens in the distance confirmed it! The firemen arrived first and hovered over Daddy checking him out. He regained consciousness at that point, but was still lying on the ground. The paramedics showed up seconds later and lifted him onto a gurney. I followed the rig in my car as they drove to the front of the building, rolled Daddy in, and handed him to the medical team.

When Daddy was checked-in and settled at Wesley Woods I went home. I was pleasantly surprised to discover that Sydney and Gracie had not pooped or torn up the house! After feeding them, I opened that backdoor so that they could run in the yard. As I stood in the doorway watching them, I replayed the past 12 hours in my head. For the most part it had been an emotional nightmare! However, I laughed out loud as I reflected on my clash of religions! If there was a God, he was upset at my ignorance and lack of faith.

As for the Buddhist part, since I was a novice, I didn't know who I had pissed off! I had tons more to learn about that! Before going to sleep, I called my brother and sister to update them.

A week passed, the snow melted, and I thought Daddy might be getting well enough to come home soon. The doctors told me that his blood pressure was under control and he would be fine. They were wrong. I don't remember the order of events, but instead of improving, his health declined. Wesley Woods transported him back to Emory Hospital. Something had gone awry and his doctors could not explain it! I maintained my composure fairly well up until the point when a nurse shoved a clipboard into my hand and asked me to make a decision about whether I wanted the medical staff to resuscitate him if he stopped breathing. Stunned, I dropped the clipboard and ran into the restroom where I burst into tears. The nurse knocked on the door and apologized for being so abrupt. I called my brother Johnny who drove in from Chicago the next day to support me. Daddy seemed better for a moment. He was talking and teasing with the nurses. Daddy told Johnny and me to cremate him if he died. We weren't worried about that because he seemed to be improving. However, I noticed Daddy's eyes. They were hazy and glossy-looking, sort of like he was wearing contacts. But he was conscious and that's all that mattered. Johnny stayed about two days then returned to Chicago on a high note. That high note was short-lived as Daddy's health took a nosedive. *What happened! I couldn't figure it out! The medical staff could not explain how he went from laughing and talking, to converting into a vegetative state!* Preparing for his death, I started looking for crematories in Atlanta.

Daddy remained unconscious for over two weeks. But just when I thought all hope was gone, something unbelievable happened! One day while I was at the hospital, a nurse called me to the phone to speak with a heart specialist who wanted to discuss Daddy's diagnosis. Up until then no one had identified his illness. The doctor explained that the chronic headaches Daddy experienced back in January were symptoms of extremely high blood pressure which resulted in a stroke. While in the hospital recovering from that, he suffered a mild heart attack but no damage was done. Maybe that's what his hazy eyes were trying to tell us. The doctor concluded with the best news of all...*Daddy's prognosis was good!* The stroke was a brain bleed and his body would re-absorb the blood allowing him to get better. Shaking my head in disbelief, I asked if he knew my dad was 83. He laughed and said, "Your father will have to go to rehab for a month to learn how to walk and talk, but he will be able to go home with you after that."

I desperately wanted to thank the doctor for his accuracy, but wondered if I had actually talked to the heart specialist or dreamed it! All I know is that his predictions came true and Daddy really did get better! At the end of February 2005, Daddy was transferred to Emory's rehabilitation center Budd Terrace. The following month he started walking, talking and gulping his food down as usual. Now my work would begin!

Reflections

- *Panic is a natural response to sudden changes!*

- *You have more courage than you think!*

Merging

I BECAME INCREASINGLY nervous as the day approached for Daddy to be released from Budd Terrace! I felt like a first-time mother bringing home her newborn! While in the hospital, nurses teach the mom how to take care of her baby. When discharged she's on her own in performing those duties! From January through March 2005, Daddy's life had been filled with doctors, nurses, nurse's aides, housekeepers, and cooks. I realize now that I had the easy part then...*visiting*! Three days before discharge, Daddy's doctor called me saying that he was ready for pick up! The doctor was thrilled that Daddy was on the mend and I was too, but how could I learn to take care of him in three short days? I would have to dispense his meds, prepare his meals, clean his room, get him dressed, wash his clothes, and much more! Like a new mom, I was about to be on my own!

This was no longer an extended visit. There was no ending date to this stay. He was sick and for the first six months Daddy lived with me, I was unforgivably angry with my mother! She had spoiled Daddy so badly that no one could ever nurture him like she had. I couldn't prepare home-cooked meals, clean a house, or iron his clothes like *she had.* I was his daughter. My role was different. The Bible only required that I love, honor, and respect him. She was his wife and had taken marriage vows to love him through sickness and health. She enjoyed the healthy part for 34 years. Mama was nine years Daddy's junior and shocked everyone by dying before him at the tender age of 61. That left me with the *sickness* part. This wasn't *my* choice! I had to modify my life to take care of him. Grandma often told me that life wasn't fair, but my ally had died in 1991, a year after Mama, so who was going to help me navigate my way through this chapter of life? It wasn't fair!

The doctor at Budd Terrance scheduled a meeting for me with the social worker to organize home-health care. That was a relief, because I didn't know where to start with such planning! The day that Daddy came home, my house became a revolving door for nurses, occupational therapists, physical therapists, and caregiver candidates. I took a vacation from work to transition Daddy into his new home. And this was now *his home.* His standard week-long visit had already been extended to three months and he was in no condition to live autonomously.

The home-health care staff was referred by the hospital, so I didn't have to interview them. Finding a caregiver to sit with him was my job and proved to be a Herculean task! He didn't like any-one! The first woman was too young. The second lady talked on her phone too much and didn't give him her undivided attention. The third lady had young children and Daddy thought she might bring the noisy brats to work, so he vetoed her! Recognizing a pattern, I realized that Daddy wanted to choose his own caregiver! He didn't want me doing it for him. There was nothing wrong with the candidates' ability to take care of him. My little cub was re-emerging as the lion king he once was and making an effort to regain his seat on the throne! I was proud of him and also wanted him to be king again, but since making this adjustment was new to me too,

I needed him to let *me* steer the way first. Daddy was determined to be in charge. *Why couldn't he just let me get things started then I would let him help! I never took care of a sick person before and had no idea what to do. I had to figure out what was best for him! Couldn't he understand that!*

Days before my vacation ended, the big picture became crystal clear! Daddy really didn't want a caregiver at all, he wanted *me!* Every time I mentioned going back to work, he would ask, "Do you *have* to go back?" Daddy had chosen me to be his rescuer just as he had been mine many years before. While I was the youngest, in his opinion I was also the bossiest! I was also the only one who was a parent. Daddy was acutely aware of parenting tasks such as planning, making tough decisions, sacrificing, and balancing work with home life. Perhaps he was confident that because I had raised two children, which became more difficult after my divorce, certainly I had the skills to help him through this phase of life. Who knows what was going through that gray-haired head of his! I didn't have a clue what was to come, but after he had been with me for six months, I recognized that raising kids was merely a precursor to raising Daddy!

I hoped our adjustment to living together in my adulthood would go smoothly simply because we loved each other. That helped, but it would require loving on a level deeper than anything I had ever experienced! It would mean putting Daddy's needs ahead of mine and not resenting it. It would mean being okay with spending money on Daddy that I had saved for something else. It would mean rearranging my new house so that he could move around in it without falling. It would mean buying him a bright, ugly, clunky oversized recliner, like the one he had in Gary so that he could feel at home. It would mean watching him toss the dogs food from his plate when I begged him not to. And it would mean finding things that he enjoyed in his new domain. Most of all, it would mean finding a way to be the leader without dethroning the king.

While Daddy had the mind of a strong independent man, his intellect competed with his physical decline. That dichotomy was frustrating and demeaning to him. Simple things like tying his shoes, getting dressed, or bathing became a challenge. Daddy would sometimes have tantrums and resort to childlike behavior. He refused to get dressed on time, making me late for work. He wouldn't eat his food and would tighten his lips and turn his back to me when pouting. I could see his pride slipping away and I had to do something!

A few minor wardrobe changes restored his confidence. We replaced his laced shoes, with shoes with Velcro fasteners. Instead of pullover shirts, which required him to lift his frail arms above his head, I bought him shirts with zippers. I converted the standard shower in his bathroom to one with a seat and a hose that he could use to lather and rinse himself. Thank goodness Mario was great at handyman tasks and remodeling! My favorite modification was buying Daddy a hearing-impaired phone so that he could talk to his friends in Gary!

The changes to accommodate Daddy's physical needs were easy, but I felt ill-equipped to deal with his strong spirit of independence. He could be stubborn and argumentative at times, though I learned it wasn't personal. He wasn't resisting my help, but instead fighting the villains called *sickness* and *old age.*

"BJ we have to find someone to stay with you because you can't stay home alone."

"Yes I can," he affirmed with authority. "The dogs are here with me."

"Sydney and Gracie can't take care of you! They can only bark!" I replied sternly.

With a few days left before returning to work, I tabled that quarrel for another time. The next morning at the post office, I found the answer to our problem. Or should I say the answer found me.

I was standing in line thinking about which stamps to buy when I heard a whisper behind me, "I'll help you take care of your dad!" *Was this like the mysterious heart specialist phone call last month? Was anyone actually standing behind me?* I made a 180-degree turn and saw my Buddhist friend Minnie. She had been a caregiver for an elderly guy whose daughter had decided to take care of him. Minnie was available to help with Daddy. However, I wasn't sure that she would be an acceptable choice – not because she wasn't a seasoned caregiver, but because I hadn't told Daddy that I was a Buddhist yet. He had already dismissed one candidate because she wanted to talk about the Bible and God all day. Daddy attended church in Gary, but wasn't the type to talk about religion incessantly, or at all! I didn't want Minnie to talk to him about Buddhism either! Since we were running low on time, I decided to give it a try. "Let me think about it and I will call you tomorrow," I told Minnie. At that moment, I remembered how to get Daddy to cooperate!

When I got home, I nervously procrastinated before talking to Daddy about Minnie. He was sitting at the card table in our small game room playing Solitaire. I walked slowly into the room and started the difficult conversation.

"BJ, I have to go back to work soon, but I have an idea," I suggested optimistically.

"What is it?" he asked suspiciously.

"I know you don't need anyone to stay home with you while I'm at work, but I would feel comfortable if someone popped in to check on you so that I would know that you're safe. Plus if you call me at work, I might be in a meeting and can't answer the phone. What do you think?" I was proud that I had presented an acceptable solution.

"How long would they stay?" he asked.

"Only a few hours. You get to decide whether you want them to come in the morning or afternoon," I offered.

There was silence. I knew that meant he was thinking it over. I had figured out the right bait to put on the hook...*give him a choice*. I remained silent as long as he did. He was pondering and I was holding my breath! After what seemed liked hours, he finally agreed. My fish was on the hook! Now came the reeling in part. Minnie came for an interview the next day and with Daddy *leading* the questioning, she was hired!

The strategy for securing Minnie as a caregiver unlocked the door to living with Daddy successfully. Many more hurdles lie ahead for both of us, but I held the key! I became masterful at guiding outcomes by letting Daddy think that he was in control. That's a tactic I learned from Mama. She told me that you could get a man to do anything you wanted by letting him think that it was *his* idea!

One Friday she told me to watch as she convinced him to take the family to the drive-in movie theatre when he didn't want to go. I think I was 8 or 9 years old. Daddy came home and tossed his suit jacket on his recliner in the living room. Mama asked where he was taking us for our Friday night outing. He told her that he was tired and didn't feel like going anywhere. The aroma of her cooking lured him to the kitchen.

"I'm sorry that you're too tired to take the kids out tonight. They are going to make a lot of noise in here!" Mama said, setting her trap.

"They won't bother me, because I'm going to take a nap!" Daddy countered.

"Diane is going to be disappointed because she really wanted to see *Pinocchio*, but you're right. You are tired and she and Johnny will just have to understand."

"How much does that movie cost?" Daddy asked as he walked out of the kitchen.

"Oh I don't know. I suppose an outing for the four of us could get pricey with buying the theatre popcorn and candy. You're not thinking about going are you?" she asked following him to the bedroom.

"Well you can take your own snacks when you go to the drive-in. We can cook our own popcorn and take it," Daddy said as if he was orchestrating everything.

"That's a great idea Honey!" she said as she strutted proudly back to the kitchen.

Mama had successfully set the trap and captured her prey! Maybe some of Mama's wit had rubbed off on me after all! To raise Daddy I would need every lesson I learned from Mama, Daddy, Grandma, and everyone else who had anything to share! Our love deepened beyond my wildest imagination, as we conquered many unforeseen obstacles along our path to role-reversal.

Reflections

- *Learn what strategies work best with whom you're working.*

- *Sometimes you already have the answers...just think!*

Tale of Two Jesses

*"It was the best of times, it was the worst of times...it was
the season of light, it was the season of darkness..."*
Charles Dickens

DADDY HAD BEEN LIVING with me about four years
when the words by Charles Dickens in *Tale of Two Cities* began to
resonate clearly...*It was the best of times, it was the worst of times.*
It was the best of times because we were so much alike. It was the
worst of times because we were so much alike. Daddy and I had
medium brown skin, round faces with high cheekbones, bright
friendly eyes, and were of average height. Family lore has it that
my mother announced her pregnancy with me was her last rodeo.
It's not like she had a bunch of children. My sister Sandra was 12
years older and she had given birth to my brother 13 months before
me. I guess Mama felt that three pregnancies in one lifetime were
enough! My brother *John* was named after her father. I was Daddy's
last chance to give their child his name regardless of gender. My
only saving grace, if you can call it that, is that he inserted an "i"
in the spelling of my name thinking that would make it feminine.
It didn't work! There were countless times in school when teachers
would call my name on the first day of class and no matter how
high I raised my hand they would say, "Where is he? Jessie are you

here?" It was enough to give a kid an esteem complex and it did! Not to mention that when I was accepted to Howard University in 1974, I was assigned to Drew Hall...a *men's dormitory*! It's been an ongoing saga of confusion thanks to Daddy!

As it turned out, Daddy and I shared more than a first name throughout life. We were school social workers. We were altruistic to a fault! We were extremely loyal to people we loved. We were accommodating and could befriend just about anyone. Utmost, we looked for the meaning and purpose in everything! Our similarities were deep and expansive, but so were our differences. Daddy smoked Dutch Masters Cigars, enjoyed all sports, thrived on a good verbal spar with anyone, was stubborn as heck, enjoyed a good brew, and had a healthy sense of humor. With the exception of a healthy sense of humor, none of those qualities describe me.

While Daddy was tremendously sensitive for the most part, there was one area in which he could be incredibly insensitive with me... my weight. I don't think it was an act of thoughtlessness as much as it was his deep-rooted attachment to society's stereotypic views of men and women. Daddy was unwavering on the double-standard that men could be overweight and attractive, but not women. Johnny was a chubby kid. We had to buy his clothes in the husky section of the Robert Hall clothing store downtown. I thought that *husky* was a brand name like Gucci, because there was no shame in buying large-size clothes for boys. I didn't put on extra weight until adulthood. Unfortunately, Daddy didn't show me the same impartiality related to size as he did my brother in his pudgy days.

The negative comments about my body started when Daddy was in the hospital. The first one came as he was recovering from his illness and was beginning to feel like his jovial old self. To prevent him from falling out of the bed, the nurses raised the side rails. They were so high that even though I stood on my toes as I leaned over to kiss him on the forehead, he had to sit up a bit to meet me halfway. He joked, "What's wrong? Are you too fat to reach me?" As he laughed, I took a deep breath and held it while seething! The sting of his comment paralyzed me for a few seconds. Since he was in the hospital, I attributed his quirky sense of humor to his sickness and let it go. But months later when he was home with me, he made a second attack on my weight to which I could not recoil. Daddy liked to check his weight and I feared he would fall off the flimsy bathroom scale if he tried to weigh himself without help. So to keep him from using it when I wasn't home, I removed it.

One day he went to the bathroom to weigh and realized that it was gone and asked, "Where is the scale?"

Trying to spare his feelings, I replied, "I don't have a scale."

"You had one in here when I came. What happened? Did you stand on it and break it?" he said in a tone that was a cross between laughter and seriousness.

What! Had he just called me fat...again? But this time he meant really fat! So much so that I could break a scale? Hurt was an understatement! I felt my anger rising like the weather on a hot July day... only much faster! I wanted to yell, "Stop it! Quit! That hurts! I inherited my body and genes from you, so how dare you call me fat! I hate when you pick on me about my weight!" But the huge lump in my throat and profound respect wouldn't let the words flow from my mouth. Tears flooded my eyes and I dashed to my bedroom to call Debbye. When I told her what Daddy had said, she protested adamantly that I could not ignore his slur this time! She convinced me that BJ was regaining his health and was strong enough for me to confront him. Debbye was certain that if I didn't strike back now, Daddy would always take shots at my weight masking them as jokes. It took about two days, but I finally mustered up the nerve to tell him that his comment about the scale hurt my feelings. At first he denied knowing what I was talking about, so I reminded him! I expected him to apologize, but instead he told me that I was too sensitive. Having calmed down significantly by then, I wasn't upset when I didn't get my apology. Sufficient for the moment was the pride I felt in being courageous enough to defend myself! For me this was a *season of light* as I had never stood up to Daddy in this manner.

Painful as it was, Daddy's criticism of my size wasn't the *worst of times*. Darker still was the physical ailments I endured from being a caregiver. I had often heard of patients who had outlived their caregivers, but I didn't understand how that reality was possible until I became the one giving long-term care. By the second year, I had gained 30 pounds, developed hypertension, and was frequently exhausted. At one point the whites of my eyes turned red…actually pink. Thinking I had a severe health issue, I frantically made an appointment to see my primary care physician to check my blood pressure. It was normal thanks to my taking a daily Diovan pill, coupled with swimming three times a week. Thinking it could be pressure building behind my eyes, my doctor referred me to an ophthalmologist. The doctor ran tests to confirm that my eye pressure was normal and then gave me a prescription for an expensive cream that only cleared my eyes for a few seconds. Moving on, I tried alternative medicine. Several herbal concoctions later, I still had reddish pink eyes. This continued for months! I wore sunglasses even indoors, because I didn't want anyone to think that I had turned to alcohol to cope with my stress. In my twenties, I had dated two heavy drinkers and both had red eyes! Surely everybody knew that red eyes meant *boozer.*

Worried that whatever was wrong with me was getting worse, I returned to my primary care physician demanding that she run some kind of test, take blood work, or do *something*! I updated her on my results from the ophthalmologist and naturopath, when she paused and asked a profound question, "Are you still taking care of your father?"

I sat quietly for a few seconds, took a deep breath, and pushed out the word, "Yes."

Dr. Begovic unfolded her arms and with a supportive touch on my shoulder smiled, "You're simply exhausted."

Really! Was that it? What an epiphany! I was relieved to learn that exhaustion could affect my health in more ways than elevated blood pressure and weight gain! I was cured! My eyes cleared the next day and the reddish pink eye never returned. My *season of darkness* was lifting.

Reflections

- *Emotional stress can present itself in physical ailments.*

- *Get regular physical checkups.*

- *Search for answers in more than one place.*

- *In the midst of demands or challenges, take a minute to breathe and reflect.*

Decisions

"Always make decisions that prioritize your inner peace."
Izey Victoria Odiase, Personal Development Advocate

ONE OF THE MOST challenging parts of taking care of Daddy was the numerous decisions I had to make on his behalf. As a parent I had made tons of decisions for my children, but there was a noticeable difference when making them for Daddy. He wanted a vote in the decision-making. I felt like he didn't trust my judgment and had to approve of my plans. Later I realized that it was one of the ways that he held on to his independence.

Most of the time I didn't mind including him in the decision for meal selections for the week or our entertainment activities, but he had proven over the years that he did not make good financial decisions. Neither did Mama for that matter. I was about 15 years old when Mama bought her first car. She enjoyed her job as a social worker assistant and was happy to be managing her own money. Mama proudly bought a car without Daddy's help. Days before her first car payment was due, she went to the post office to mail it. It would take about two to three business days for the check to travel to the finance company for processing before working its way to the bank. The same day Mama dropped the payment in the mail, she called the bank to check her balance...this was years before online banking. Of course the money for the car payment was still there, because the check had not yet traveled through the mail to the finance company. Happy to hear the balance in her account, off she went to the mall to buy shoes, matching purses, and anything else she desired. Even at age 15, and with below average math skills, I knew something was wrong with that logic. Needless to say by the time the finance company sent the check to the bank, that money was gone. Mama angrily blamed the bank for her lack of sufficient funds to cover the car payment. Daddy's strategies were much the same.

I knew managing money was a decision I would have to make without his input! His mental faculties were intact, so he would notice that I was deliberately *not* discussing money matters with him. I would have to out-think him on this. In a workshop I attended on caregiving, the presenter told us to include the *caregivee* in the planning of their lives as much as possible to show love, care, open communication, and to provide the caregivee a sense of security and value. Seeing the financial muddle Daddy had created with his finances, I didn't see how much help he could be in organizing, but I gave it a shot. After dinner one evening, we sat at his game table and I placed all his papers in stacks. He smiled as if he thought we were getting ready to play a game. I started the conversation, "Daddy we need to sort things out, so that we can pay your bills." The smile disappeared as quickly as it came when he saw the mound of papers on the table.

"Is that what all that is?"

"Yes Daddy. We need to look at due dates, minimum amounts due, and start paying things. Some accounts are late because I didn't pay them when you were in the hospital."

"You figure it out Miss Jessie."

With that last comment, he got up from the table and went into the living room to watch TV. *How dare he leave me with this disaster! Like it or not I had to get to work!*

Notebooks and folders were my best friends for organizing my finances, so I got some for Daddy too. It took a few days, but I eventually sorted out the Visa, MasterCard, and American Express statements. I made folders for every account. There were three gas credit cards, Shell, Amoco, and Phillips 66. Also in the mix were department store cards. Sears, J.C. Penney's, and L.S. Ayers had the highest balances. He was drowning in debt. I had no sympathy for merchants who extended credit cards with high limits to seniors on fixed incomes. Since we had sold his house, I only saw one way out...bankruptcy. Making that decision was easy. The next step was discussing my plan with Daddy. I couldn't file bankruptcy without his approval and input. My approach was not to ask for his help, but to tell him how this was going down!

Armed with my notebooks and folders, I met with Daddy again. This time I showed him his expenses and income in an orderly fashion. He couldn't argue that his finances were in bad shape! I told him that he could not continue to live on cash advances, then ask the credit companies to increase his limit...which they gladly did.

"How did things get so bad Miss Jessie?"

"Don't worry Daddy, I have a plan to clean this up and give you more money to live on. You wanna know what I think?"

"Yeah, what do you think?'

I had to be careful not to make him think that he had made poor decisions and wrecked his life. He still needed to feel like a king and have his dignity intact.

"Well Daddy, first of all the credit companies prey on seniors by extending them lots of credit. They knew that you weren't working when they sent you all those cards. So what do you think about wiping the slate clean with all of them?"

"How can we do that?" he sounded interested and didn't bolt for the TV.

With a lump in my throat I answered, "By filing bankruptcy."

There was a long silence as he pondered my idea, "Bankrupt? You mean I'd be broke?"

"No Daddy you would finally have your money back! You wouldn't be broke and I could help you keep your money."

"Would they take my Social Security and pension?"

"Nope! You would get to keep all of that!"

Relieved that bankruptcy wouldn't affect his income or health benefits, he was all in! Daddy liked the sound of having money again. He trusted me to fix things for him.

In less than six months, we cleared his debt! I routed his Social Security and Teacher Retirement Pension into joint accounts with me. I gave him a monthly allowance of $400 and paid for bingo and casino trips. The rest of the money helped with household expenses, buying him clothes, and opening a small savings account. The king was back on his throne with money in his pocket!

Reflections

- *If the person you are caring for is a senior, you must organize their affairs. If they are lucid, do so in a way that empowers them.*

- *You will need their permission to discuss their accounts with creditors, so arrange that as soon as possible. It will involve phone calls or letters. Email communication may also be an option.*

- *Always be gentle when you criticize.*

- *Allow caregivees to retain dignity.*

Suspensions

ONCE OUR ROUTINE WAS solidified, I was able to slow my pace and focus some attention back on myself…or so I thought! Realizing that Daddy was not at the end of his life, I did not have to invest 200% of my energy into making sure that his last year or two were his happiest. He was getting stronger each day while I was wearing down!

Swimming three times a week was my stress relief. I begin to look thinner too, even though the scale never changed. I would come home from work, feed Daddy, and then go to the pool for an hour. This hour happened to be during our *Wheel of Fortune* time and he didn't like that one bit! The pool closed at 8:00 in the evening, so I had to chop off some TV time to get there and back before closing. When I packed my gym bag and headed toward the door, I always said, "See you later BJ." Instead of returning the comment he'd ask me if I really had to go. I ignored him and continued to the car. *How could he be so selfish! I took him to bingo Wednesday, Friday, and Saturday! Why couldn't I swim Monday, Tuesday, and*

Thursday? I thought he wanted me to exercise since he took jabs at my weight every chance he got!

If a weight loss commercial came on while we were watching TV, he would ask, "Have you tried that before?" If there was a 2-for-1 special at a gym, he laughed, "Do you have a friend that you can take to that?" I didn't find it funny at all. My profound respect for him muted my tongue when he said hurtful things. I mumbled inaudibly, "Yeah, I can take you!" Knowing my father, I knew we were only revisiting the double-standard of beauty that he accepted. Women were not attractive if they were heavy. While he commented mostly on my size, he made more subtle comments about women who had light skin being prettier than those with darker complexions. For the record, I had his skin color and bone structure. My mother was his standard of beauty. Light skin, long soft hair, thin, curvy hips, and big shapely legs. I inherited my mom's curvy hips and shapely legs, but everything else was all from Daddy!

That takes me to the next thing I didn't do much of...dating. I seldom went out before he came to live with me, but seldom became *never*! On one of our trips to the Veterans Administration (VA) Hospital a man was flirting with me in the waiting area. At least I think he was. He seemed like a decent man. My perspective beau was reasonably nice-looking, tall, and muscular. His age was probably early 50s. When the man asked me any question, Daddy rudely interrupted and changed the subject. *How could he even hear what the guy was saying because he wasn't shouting? Maybe Daddy's hearing loss wasn't as severe as he pretended.* The gentleman gave up trying to start up a conversation with me and resorted to flirting with his eyes and a smile. I found myself batting my lashes at him! Daddy spotted me doing that too! He was not going to stand for such behavior. "Di go get me some water," he demanded sternly. I took a deep breath, rolled my eyes, and then complied. By the time I returned, the guy was gone. Who knows whether he was called in to see the doctor or whether Daddy told him to get lost! I figured that Daddy was protecting his interest…me as his caregiver. Maybe he saw something in that guy that was shady. I didn't. Who knows what it was! I never saw that man again.

The next guy I met was through a mutual friend. The first thing he commented on was how attractive I was. A stark contrast to Daddy's view of me. We met for lunch a few times and went to dinner twice. Since Daddy was a large part of my life, he was often the center of my conversations. At times when I vented about something Daddy had done that upset me, he would say, "I don't know why you put up with that crap from him! *Crap? I never considered anything Daddy did as crap? Exhausting yes. Insensitive yes. But crap, never!* The final straw with this guy was when he asked me if I wanted to go on a trip somewhere. I think it was Hawaii. *Was he kidding? How was I supposed to make arrangements for caregiving for an extended period of time?* I told him that I had obligations and couldn't do it. He looked at me and said, "If I was you, I'd toss his butt in a nursing home." I wasn't tossing him anywhere! He was my father and I loved him! No one could grate my nerves more than Daddy. He could wear me out with his elderly demands, but I was in charge of his care! I was *his* protector! That was my mission! The source of great love…Daddy, was also the source of great pain. That's just human nature! In hindsight, that man at the VA was never meant to be a keeper…just a messenger. The message was that *Daddy was the center of my world.*

Other activities that took a lengthy hiatus during my caregiving stage of life were writing, leisure reading, going to work-related activities after hours, and attending outings with friends. I accepted that. My life was now an extension of his. It was less stressful to view life that way. In my heart, I knew that one day my activities would be restored.

Reflections

- *When you love someone, putting their needs first is natural.*

Balancing Act

"Don't let anyone convince you that you owe them an explanation."
Unknown

LIKE A CLOWN, I FELT like I was juggling bowling pins. As I tossed the pins in the air attempting to catch them without dropping one, I would drop one...or two!

I panicked when I dropped one because it meant I had failed at my job of protecting Daddy. Two vivid examples come to mind.

On our trips to the Veterans Administration (VA) Hospital, I would park the car, get out, then walk around to the passenger's side to help Daddy climb out. Together we walked through the circuitous hallway to the elevators, which we rode up to the 10th floor to the Bronze Unit. We walked the same path each visit passing the information desk, library, and the wall of pictures featuring war heroes. As soon as I checked him in on the Bronze Unit, he had to go to the restroom. I took him a few times, before he eventually told me that he knew how to get there without me. He couldn't get lost because if he passed the restroom, he would circle back to the nurse's station and waiting area. Either a nurse or I would spot him and assist if needed. In his usual saving face manner, he denied being lost and said he was just getting in some exercise before seeing the doctor. Eventually, he learned his way to the restroom and back to the waiting area. Watching him gain confidence becoming independent at the VA was right up there with the pride parents feel watching their babies take their first steps!

My confidence was shattered and my heart raced in fear, the day Daddy broke our routine. This particular day the parking lot was full, and I had to circle around numerous times waiting for someone to vacate a space. Since parking took longer than usual, Daddy had to go to the restroom before I could park the car. No way was I sending him into that large building with no escort. The longer I circled around the parking lot, the stronger he insisted that he had to go to the restroom.

"Di, let me out! I know how to get to the restroom," he shouted.

"Just wait Daddy. I'll be parked in a second," I tried to assure him.

"Let me out in front! I know my way!"

My heart was racing. *Dammit, he doesn't know his way! If I let him out, he's going to get lost. But if he doesn't get to a restroom soon, he's going to pee in my car! Where was someone who could help me?* I wanted to cry, but instead I pounded on the steering wheel in frustration as I decided to let him out at the front door. Maybe he would ask someone at the information desk to direct him to the nearest restroom…I hoped. So against everything I was feeling, I dropped him off at the curb and watched him hobble with his cane to the front door. Back I went to the parking area circling for another 15 minutes before finding a space. I leaped out of the car and dashed to the information desk where I asked the lady sitting there if she had seen an old man wearing a baseball hat. She chuckled and said, "Ma'am look around." There were old men walking with canes and wearing baseball caps all around us! *How would I ever find Daddy?* At that moment, I felt like the mother who while playing with her child at the park, turned her head for a second and the child disappeared. *There were tons of restrooms in the VA! Which one had he gone to? Did he find his way up to the Bronze Unit? Probably not, because I always pressed the elevator button, so he wouldn't know what floor it was on.* I just started walking through the halls in hopes of finding him. It felt like I was walking in slow motion. Feeling completely inadequate as a *parent* I couldn't think clearly. The only feelings I experienced were fear, confusion, and anger at myself for going against my better judgment! I was a failure as a parent to my father! What kind of person was I to risk losing my 84-year-old father instead of letting him pee in the car? I was the pits!

Just when I was about to go back to the information desk to ask them to page him or whatever they needed to do to find a lost veteran, I looked up and there he was! I squinted my eyes to make sure that it wasn't an illusion. The cowboys did that in the movies when they were thirsty for water and spotted a mirage of a puddle. When they ran to the perceived puddle of water it was nothing but sand! I wasn't sure if Daddy was real or a mirage stemming from my thirst to find him! This mirage was walking toward me waving his hand. It had to be him! No one else at the VA knew me or would be happy to see me! As Daddy approached me he was sporting a smile like we were seeing each other for the first time in years! At that moment I didn't know if he had found the restroom or not, but I knew he had gotten lost! Daddy would never admit it. I didn't care if he ever confessed to being lost, I had found him…and was NEVER going to lose him again!

That promise lasted until my father's friend from college came to visit. I don't remember the length of time between losing Daddy at the VA and his friend's visit, but obviously enough time had passed that I forgot my promise! My father's friend Sam was visiting his daughter in Atlanta and they wanted to take Daddy to lunch. They invited me too, but yearning for some alone time, I declined. I explained to Sam's daughter Carol that Daddy was diabetic and had dietary restrictions. She assured me that it would not be a problem.

Daddy was so excited to be going to lunch with his college buddy Sam that he barely finished his breakfast! Sam and Carol were late, but Daddy wouldn't even let me give him a snack. They arrived an hour later. Releasing a sigh of relief, I waved as they left. Now I had a few hours to myself! *What would I do with free time?* I hopped in the tub for a relaxing bubble bath! Next, I danced to some oldies as I did a little housecleaning. An hour had passed. The phone rang. Daddy was on the other end. "Come get me Di," he said in a disgusted voice.

"What happened Daddy?"

"Carol left us here and said that she would be right back. I'm hungry, come get me!"

"Why are you hungry? Didn't you go to lunch?"

"Not yet! Just come get me!"

"Daddy where are you?"

"I don't know. Carol brought us to her house and said she had to run an errand first. She's not back yet."

This was déjà vu of the harrowing VA experience! Daddy did not know where he was and neither did I!

I frantically called Carol's cell, but she did not answer. I paced the floor like an expectant father! I banged my hands against my head! *Why did I let her take him out of my sight! I should have demanded to go to lunch with them, but instead I opted for a few hours of solitude! Stupid! Stupid! Stupid! I didn't deserve to be Daddy's caregiver! Twice I failed to protect him! If I ever got him back, I would watch him like a hawk!*

Within about 30 minutes, Carol brought him home with a burger in a bag. *What happened? What on earth was more important than feeding two old men?*

"Carol I thought you were taking them to lunch!"

"I decided they would like to just sit and talk without me around, so I dropped them off at my house and ran some errands!" she replied calmly.

"That's not what you said! You were going to take them to lunch! I told you that my dad is diabetic and *has* to eat on a schedule!" I said firmly, but low enough for our dads not to hear my disgust with her.

"I forgot," she giggled.

What in the hell was funny about this situation? Couldn't she read my body language? I was so angry with her that I wanted to slap her...and I have never slapped anyone!

I could see that Daddy's blood sugar had dropped by his weak walk. He didn't want me to be angry with Carol, so he sat at the table, quickly gobbled his hamburger, and told me how much he enjoyed seeing Sam again. I'm glad he did, because he was never going to visit Sam or anyone else without me in tow!

We never spoke of that incident again! It was scary for both of us!

That was the second and final time I dropped my pins while juggling! I don't care how stressful taking care of Daddy could get, I would never choose my needs such as maintaining a clean car and having some free time over Daddy's safety. No good parent would put their child in harm's way. And I did...*twice*! I vowed never to let anyone talk me into letting Daddy out of my sight again!

Reflections

- *You don't owe anyone an explanation for the choices you make... especially as it relates to someone you are responsible for!*

- *Improve on what doesn't work well...don't beat yourself up about it.*

Myrt

Every Man for Himself
Proverbs

I ENJOYED DADDY staying in touch with his old friends as much as he did. But one day his connection sent shock waves through my body as I had to tactfully find a way to decline a request from one of them. Saturday morning he would call his friends. I listened from another room as he laughed and teased with former neighbors, fraternity brothers, church members, and coworkers. Most of his conversations ended with, "Okay, I'll tell Di you said hi." But this particular call ended with, "Okay, I'll ask Di." *What on earth was he going to ask me?*

Unable to wait for him to approach me, I walked briskly into his room still wiping my hands on the dishcloth from washing dishes and asked, "You're going to ask me what? Who was that on the phone?"

"Myrt wants to come visit us," he coolly replied as he continued flipping the pages in his phonebook looking for the next friend to call. Myrtle or Myrt as he called her, fit into two categories in his life. She was a former classmate and coworker, which doubled his affinity for her! Daddy had been good friends with Myrt's late husband and had remained in contact with her since they graduated from high school. I met Myrt and knew her children. She was always nice to me, but I couldn't figure out why she wanted to visit with us when two of her children also lived in Atlanta. Maybe I had jumped to conclusions. Perhaps she was not planning to stay at our house, but coming to visit her children and only intended to pop in to have dinner with us one evening. Checking out my hope, I relaxed and calmly asked Daddy, "Oh that would be great to see her again when she comes to town to see her family! When is she coming?" He told me to call her to find out.

That's when the butterflies in my stomach started stirring around like crazy! How could I tell her that she simply could not stay with us! Two people like Daddy exceeded my limits of caregiving! Before calling Myrt, I did a few practice runs in front of the mirror.

- *Hey Myrt! Daddy told me you were coming to town to visit your boys. When will you be here?*

- *Myrt I don't cook much, so tell me what you like to eat so I can find a nice restaurant.*

- *Myrt how many people will you bring to dinner when you stop by?*

I figured that one of these openings would be a good way to let Myrt know that I was considering this a *visit only*!

Daddy was still on the phone making calls, so I returned to the kitchen to finish washing the breakfast dishes. I wanted him to forget Myrt's request by the time he finished his Saturday phone call routine. He didn't.

He yelled from his room, "Hey Di, I'm off the phone! You can call Myrt now!" Sure I *could*, but I didn't want to. My strategy was still a work in progress. I yelled back, "Okay, I'll do it in a few minutes." Those few minutes turned into three days! He kept nudging me like a puppy who wants to play until I ran out of excuses for delaying the call.

When I called Myrt, she was delighted to hear from me, "Hey Diane, I am so glad you called! I told your dad that I wanted to come see you guys!"

"Yes Myrt he told me. When will you be in town? I'll make sure to bring him to see you or take you out to dinner or something," I feigned excitement. My contrived gesture quickly changed to full blown terror when she clarified that she was coming to spend some time with *us*! I coughed as if something were stuck in my throat, *"Us Myrt?" Oh no, this just couldn't be! Myrt wanted to stay with us and pop in on her children! That couldn't happen. I couldn't even dream about that possibility! Myrt was Daddy's age, needed a walker, and took as many pills as Daddy! There was no way that I could take care of two elderly folks. Where would she sleep? Did she have food restrictions? Not to mention that "spend some time with us" meant no designated end to her visit! I think Daddy made living with me sound so good that Myrt wanted a taste of his good life! I had many trials with Daddy, but this would be the granddaddy of them all... telling his friend NO!*

I don't remember how I concluded my conversation with Myrt, but I'm sure I was pleasant, yet never committed to a date. Daddy didn't know that I had called Myrt, so I had time to think about how to mention it to him. My first reaction was to call Myrt's family to discuss it with them, but I vaguely remember him telling me that she didn't get along well with her kids and in-laws. I was overthinking this! Myrt was in her 80s like Daddy. Maybe she would forget about the whole thing. She didn't! She called weekly asking when I had scheduled her visit. I stalled with work-related excuses for my indecisiveness until I had no choice but to involve Daddy.

When I told Daddy about Myrt's plan, he said he had no idea that she wanted to stay in our house. By the look of frustration on my face and the restrained tone of my voice, Daddy knew I was in *panic* mode! He instantly went into *protection* mode. Without saying a word, he stared out of the window in deep thought as if pondering his next chess move. Daddy knew that he had a good thing! He loved living with me, the pups, and Mario. We had our routines of weekly bingo, monthly casino trips, and watching our favorite TV shows. If Myrt came, he would have to share *our* time with her. He had to formulate a plan to rescue me from his pal without damaging their friendship. But if he couldn't succeed at both, then Myrt was out! Daddy regained his focus and told me not to worry and that he would call her to straighten things out.

I never learned what Daddy said to Myrt, because he called her while I was at work. All I know is that we never heard from Myrt again! Being a sensitive guy who valued his friends, I am positive that he didn't say anything offensive like, *Di doesn't want you to come*! Daddy genuinely felt bad that Myrt didn't have a great relationship with her family, but he couldn't repair that. He could protect himself and our family! Problem-solving and being in control were two of his outstanding qualities. The Myrt situation allowed me to be dependent on him for an answer and he did not disappoint!

Daddy never told me what he said to Myrt that ended her phone calls to me and hopes of visiting us. I believe that he fabricated a story. He probably said to her, "Myrt, I'd love for you to come, but Di has decided to move me into a nursing home." Myrt was already living in one, so she wouldn't want to move to Atlanta to do the same thing. Whatever story he created, Myrt was history! *Checkmate*!

Reflections

- *Doing something extremely well can be a curse!*

- *Sometimes you lie to spare someone else's feelings.*

- *Be prepared for your loved ones to toss the ball to you, when they don't want to be seen as unkind.*

Respite

"Be there for others, but never leave yourself behind."
Dodinsky, Author

AS MUCH AS I NEEDED a short break from caregiving, I couldn't force myself to take a respite. I was like a mother with a newborn who refused to leave her child for any reason! Daddy was my infant and as exhausting as cooking, cleaning, sorting medicine, scheduling doctor appointments, and other caring chores could be I didn't trust anyone to keep him other than myself. Thank goodness in time I learned to trust my son Mario with some caregiving responsibilities.

Daddy pouted like a toddler when I attempted to find some social activities for him. I started with the senior day care at church. He refused to go with me to visit because he didn't envision himself as an old person. Next, I tried a community senior day care. It had a pool, cafeteria, and scheduled activities like bingo and card games. Daddy loved card games, so surely this was the place! Not! At least he got out of the car to go in, but he sat in a chair and never moved. I walked around the facility with the activity coordinator, while Daddy sat shooting mean stares at us. *What was wrong with him?* The coordinator smiled and referred me to another day care that he might like. Daddy didn't even get out of the car when we got there! I was so embarrassed that I wanted to cry! When we returned home, I was tempted to scold him for acting childish. I didn't.

After an hour or so of reflecting on why he objected so vehemently to something that I was trying to do for his happiness, the epiphany appeared. Daddy was thinking that I was trying to slip him into a nursing home! All of these senior day care places looked like nursing homes. From that point on, my research included activities that we could do together...which defeated the purpose of respite, but eradicated his fears and lowered my frustration.

Maybe I needed help in coping with my new role as caregiver of my father, so I decided to seek therapy. I found a woman therapist who was in her 40s. I told her that I was seeking counseling to help with caregiver stress. I explained that I couldn't leave my father with anyone else, thus making him completely dependent on me. And that was exhausting! The therapist took out a clipboard with a form on it and started asking me a series of questions including:

How long have you lost interest in the things that you liked?
Do you use drugs?
Do you feel hopeless?
Do you want to be alone?
Are you having mood swings?

These were questions to assess my risk for suicide! *I wasn't suicidal, just tired! Didn't she read my information sheet? I listed my occupation as social worker. She should have known that I would recognize a suicide risk assessment survey when I heard one.*

The therapist irritated me with her lack of understanding! She hadn't asked one question about Daddy or the things that made me feel fatigued. She asked if anyone else lived at home. I told her my son Mario lived on campus at Tuskegee University, but came home most weekends. From there she asked if my son was a source of stress. *Why was she avoiding asking me about Daddy?* Obviously, the woman knew nothing about caregiver stress and what options to suggest. We were only 30 minutes into our 50-minute session when I decided to let her off the hook. I dug out the car key from my purse, stood up, and thanked her for her time. She asked if I wanted to schedule a second appointment. I replied, "No thanks. I'm good."

Self-care, which wasn't *a thing* at the time, was my only solution. I would have to find my own methods to rejuvenate. They are listed below.

Screaming – When I needed to release tons of stored up emotions, I went into the garage, sat in the car, and yelled as loudly as possible! A variation of this technique was to drive the car around the block while screaming! Both worked.

Bathroom Spa – I didn't like real spas, so I converted my bathroom into a 30-minute getaway. I lit scented candles, turned out the lights, played music, and soaked in a bubble bath for half an hour. The water got too cold to enjoy after that length of time. By closing my eyes, I could soar to any place my imagination could take me. This was energizing and affordable. The cost of bubble bath and candles was less than twenty dollars!

Watching TV – I did this at night when the house was quiet. Daddy and the dogs were asleep and I could enjoy a good movie. The only downside with this option was unhealthy midnight snacking.

Reading – Books and magazines were good company at the end of an exhausting day. I preferred gossip magazines and comic books to scholarly works.

Listening to music – This was easy to do while riding in the car.

These activities provided the moments of respite I needed to recharge from taking care of Daddy. I probably needed longer activities, but this was the best I could do at the time.

Reflections

- *Seeking help with caregiving does not make one weak.*

- *Taking care of self is not selfish.*

- *Therapy may offer support if the counselor understands caregiver stress.*

- *Find something to do that relaxes you. Do it often.*

- *If you don't take care of yourself, you cannot take care of others.*

Traditions

"Tradition is a guide and not a jailer."
W. Somerset Maugham, Playwright

WHEN I WAS A CHILD, my family celebrated holidays with "Jenkins Traditions." Our season started in October with Halloween, followed by Thanksgiving, Christmas, and New Year's Eve. My children and I had "Harvey Traditions" which resembled the Jenkins Traditions, but with some modifications...the main one being cuisine. I don't cook! Now that Daddy was living with us, it was imperative to keep things that were important to him and blend those with our newly created practices.

Halloween

Old: Daddy bought candy on his way home from work on Halloween. I don't know why he didn't buy it earlier, but he enjoyed stopping at the store on the same day, then dashing home before dark. My mother picked up the relay baton from there and dumped the bite-size pieces of gum and caramel candy in a bowl and placed it on a TV tray by the door. She positioned her chair next to the TV tray and was ready to welcome the cadre of costumed kids who were en route! My mother was thrilled to distribute candy and smile at the neighborhood children, pretending not to know who they were. "I wonder who that is behind the Casper the Ghost mask?" she would tease. The costumes of those days consisted of hard as heck plastic masks with flimsy satin capes or pants. The eyes and nose were cut out of the masks, so that children could breathe. Even with those holes, breathing was challenging! The costumed-cuties rang the doorbell in the evening between 6:00 and 8:00. By 8:05 we closed the door and turned out the porch light, which signaled to any late comers, *we're done!*

New: Daddy assumed Mama's role of sitting at the door distributing candy in a bowl positioned on a TV tray. The costumes changed over the years and consisted of more outlandish makeup and clothes. Tricker-treaters dressed as fairies, super heroes, ballerinas, movie villains, and some just came as they were with bag in hand! There was no need to ring the doorbell, because Daddy sat at the door looking as children walked up to the house. He had a handful of candy to give to everyone! If older siblings were escorting them, he gave them candy too. Once a little girl had her dog with her. Daddy made me run to the kitchen to get one of our dogs' treat to give to the pooch. I sat back in awe of Daddy having so much fun with the neighbors. We also started at 6:00 and by 8:00, I was ready to close the door and turn out the porch light. Daddy protested, "Stop, I see a few more kids coming." I was ready to watch a movie, but he insisted that we host a few more children. I acquiesced, but at 8:30...I was done.

Thanksgiving

Old: House impeccably clean, my mother's Thanksgiving food preparation started a week early. She cooked sweet potato pies and put them in the freezer. She made at least 12, and gave them to anyone who praised her cooking. She also cooked a 24-pound frozen turkey which took two days to thaw. The day before, she was preparing the mac and cheese, mashed potatoes, corn bread, greens, dressing, and other fixins. The night before, she started cooking the turkey which took about 12 hours. She got up throughout the night to base and turn it so that it was succulent and brown all over. Thanksgiving morning, Mama jumped out of bed at 5:00 to set the table. By the time family members arrived at noon and we sat down to eat, my mother was exhausted! I remember being angry at folks for coming to eat, but not helping to prepare the massive meal! After eating, the women sat in the kitchen smoking cigarettes and gossiping, while the men went downstairs to drink liquor and loudly tell exaggerated stories about their jobs! When all the guests were gone, I asked my mother, "Why don't you make them bring something?" She told me to mind my own business.

New: House dusted and mopped in visible areas only, I started planning what to serve a few days before Thanksgiving. I knew how much Daddy liked the traditional Thanksgiving meal, but my kids and I had long dropped that practice. It was normal for us to have pizza or seafood on Thanksgiving and Christmas. I thought that an alternative was to buy turkey slices, a small ham, and a sweet potato soufflé from the Honey Baked Ham store. Daddy thought that food was awful and was disappointed that I didn't slave over a stove for a week preparing a home-cooked festive meal. Attempting to compromise, I ordered a Thanksgiving meal from caterers. To Daddy that was a step up from Honey Baked Ham, but it wasn't Mama's cooking. Without her doing it, it was never going to be Mama's cooking! We had no extended family members coming over to hang out after the meal. This was turning into a boring holiday for Daddy. I couldn't gather up any family members, but I knew how to put the spark back in this holiday...*going to the casino*! Our new ritual became eating a catered dinner, then dashing to the Cherokee Casino in North Carolina. It couldn't replace women smoking in the kitchen or men drinking and talking loudly in the basement, but it made him just as happy!

Christmas

Old: Buy gifts for *everyone* and repeat the meal ritual from Thanksgiving! Added to this holiday was dragging out our artificial Christmas tree from the basement and decorating it with red and green breakable bulbs. We added more bulbs each year until you could see more decorations than tree. No matter how many bulbs were on the tree, Daddy added candy canes for the final touch. Grandma had extra bottles of Avon bubble bath for us to wrap and put under the tree in case unexpected friends dropped by.

New: The catered meal from Thanksgiving became a permanent practice. Instead of driving to the casino, we went to bingo on Christmas Eve. We also bought gifts for *everyone* and instead of people dropping by our house, we went to their homes to deliver them. We even had gifts for our bingo friends, which we exchanged on Christmas Eve. I was stunned at the number of people who had gifts for Daddy. The bingo crowd really loved him! Remembering what Grandma taught, I had extra items for people who gave us gifts that we hadn't included on our list. We also had gifts for the doctors, physical therapists, and friends at the local bar-and-grill where Minnie and Daddy hung out. I preferred a live Christmas tree to an artificial one. Daddy enjoyed decorating it just as much as a fake one. Gracie would drink the water from the tree container and Sydney would pull off a few ornaments. I was constantly fussing at them, but that added some spice to the holiday. Of course the topping on the tree was not the star or the angel, but the candy canes!

New Year's Eve was welcomed in with watching the countdown on TV. After that we were sleepy and went to bed! That didn't differ much from my youth. The only change was that Daddy no longer discharged his pistol. As a child, he told me that firing a gun at the stroke of midnight was symbolic of shooting out the old year to make room for the new one. His arthritis prevented him from pulling the trigger on his Smith & Wesson. Watching football on New Year's Day continued to dominate the day's activities in my past and present.

We always celebrated birthdays with the person's favorite cake and ice cream. It didn't matter how many gifts a family member received or doing whatever their favorite activity was, Mama said it wasn't an official birthday without cake and ice cream. We continued that practice when Daddy came here.

If the person you are caring for had to relocate from their home to yours, you may experience some clashes around traditions and celebrations. Make the transition as fun as possible by merging ideas to create new traditions. Include the caregivee in the new plan!

Reflections

- *It is important to allow people to keep as much of their enjoyable traditions as possible.*

- *Blending and creating traditions can be fun for everyone and help with adjustment to a new environment.*

Fireside Chats

*"Sometimes you never will know the value of a
moment until it becomes a memory."*
Dr. Seuss

BEFORE DADDY CAME to live with me, I had envisioned him moving here someday. I pictured us watching TV, playing card games, visiting friends, taking after dinner walks through the neighborhood, and enjoying chatting about life. By the time he moved here, his health prohibited some of my plans, but quiet moments for chatting popped up unexpectantly!

One of our recurring topics was marriage. Admiring the 36-year marriage that he and my mom shared made me long for such a union. My 5-year marriage was turbulent and unsatisfying. At the end of each year, I called my mother asking what to do. At the end of the first year she said, "It's only been a year. You need time to adjust." After the second year, she said, "It's just been two years. Give it more time." Things hadn't changed much in the third year and her advice was, "Well, marriage can be challenging. This is the rough part, things will get better." In the fourth year, we adopted our children. Mama's uplifting words were, "Things will definitely get better now." She was wrong. After the fifth year, the marriage was unsalvageable. I called Mama to tell her that we were divorcing.

I thanked her for her years of advice, but I was done! Her reply was, "I'm glad! I don't like him anyway!"

"Then why did you encourage me to work things out all these years?"

"Because I am your mother and that was my job. You gave it all you had, now you can leave in peace."

I believe I could have found peace by leaving that relationship sooner than five years!

As I told Daddy about that experience with Mama, I asked him if he thought I'd ever be married for 25 years. He said, "Of course you will!" Several years later, I asked if he thought I would be married for 20 years. Again he replied, "Of course you will!" Three more years passed without even a date! Once more, I asked Daddy if he thought I would be married for 15 years. To that question he replied, "Miss Jessie, you're going in the wrong direction! Your years of marriage keep decreasing."

"Yeah but my age keeps increasing!" I retorted. He smiled and assured me that I would marry again one day and be very happy!

Another popular topic was money...of which we had opposing views. I envisioned making it and saving as much as possible to sustain me after retirement. His philosophy was that you couldn't take it with you when you died, so he spent it as fast as he earned it. He and Mama shared that view. They had not saved a dime in 36 years of marriage! They had lots of fun, but no savings. In hindsight they had it right! I have a few dollars in savings, but have not had much fun!

After my divorce I never received any of the court-ordered child support payments from my ex. I worked full-time and occasionally part-time to support my two children, two dogs, and the expenses of home, car, and daily life!

One night as we sat in the rocking chairs on the deck stargazing, I said, "Daddy I want to be a millionaire. I don't want to be a social worker forever. I want to write stories, plays, and maybe even a movie or two." Without ever having read anything I wrote, he smiled and replied, "You'll do it."

Our other chats included talking about our friends, current events, and things that Daddy believed I was finally old enough to know.

Reflections

- *There are valuable nuggets in the midst of trials. Cherish them!*

Farewells and Goodbyes

"How lucky am I to have something that makes saying goodbye so hard."
Winnie the Pooh

THE SKY WAS dark gray as the vicious tornado ripped through our neighborhood dismantling everything in its wake! Trash cans were flying in the air and trees were falling like dominoes. The neighborhood itself was spinning around like a carnival ride. The neighbors to our left, the Williams family, stuffed a few suitcases in their car and drove off hurriedly. The torrential rain pounded so heavily on the back car window that I could barely see the two young daughters wave goodbye to me as their father drove directly into the tornado! The car and the Williamses vanished instantly as the community continued to swirl. Thank goodness I woke up from that heart-pounding dream, or should I say *nightmare*! I felt an intense sense of loss. It was a *goodbye* since my neighbors disappeared into the storm, never to be seen again. I was living in Atlanta when I had that nightmare about my neighborhood in Gary. It was months before Daddy came to live with me. Obviously it was a premonition of sudden goodbyes to come within the next few months.

My mother had distinct definitions of *farewells* and *goodbyes*. A *farewell* or *so long* meant that you would separate from someone, but you could see each other again. A *goodbye* was final.

This nightmare definitely symbolized a *goodbye*! Why did a tornado destroy our neighborhood as I watched from my bedroom window? Why did the Williamses drive into obscurity? I had no idea why they were the only family I recognized in the storm. Maybe because of all our neighbors, they lived the closest to us.

Mr. Williams and Daddy became friends when they moved next door to us in the early 1960s. Daddy called him *Preacher.* Both worked for the school system and spent evenings sitting on the porch discussing the business of education! Mrs. Williams was a teacher and my mother also worked for the school system, but porch-talks were exclusively for the men! One obvious reason was that the women were in the house preparing dinner for the family!

When Daddy came to live with me, no one knew it would be for the remainder of his life. Once his health declined and I knew that his independent living days were over, the dream became clear. The abrupt separation from the life he had known created a shake-up like the tornado ripping through our neighborhood. Separating from neighbors, family, and friends was a *farewell*, because they had a chance to see each other again. Daddy would have to say farewell… and later goodbye to some of his lifelong friends as he relocated to Atlanta. I won't list them all, but the few I highlight will give you an idea of what that was like for Daddy…and me. First the *farewells.*

Marilyn and Family

Marilyn was Daddy's *special friend.* They had an extraordinary friendship wherein they shared secrets, fun moments, hardships, and a profound respect for each other. When Daddy decided to return home with me, Marilyn was the first person he called with the news. She in turn called her adult daughters, who had grown to know and love Daddy too. The whole crew came by to say farewell to Daddy. I begged them not to cry, so he wouldn't get upset, but

I learned that request was too much to ask of them. I didn't know for sure that Daddy would eventually move to Atlanta, but I guess on some level we all knew. The good news is that they could visit with him. I'm happy to report that they did!

Mr. Williams

Realizing that Atlanta was now his new residence, we decided to sell his house in Gary. When we flew to Gary to close the sale of the house, Mr. Williams was in a nursing home. He had lost his mobility and his memory was sporadic. We asked Mrs. Williams if we could go see him while we were in town. She cheerfully gave us her approval, but cautioned that if he wasn't having a good day, he might not know us. A sadness fell over me like a blanket. *What if Mr. Williams didn't recognize us as we showed up to say so long?* That was a thought too painful to bear, so I dismissed it. I took a deep breath and shook it off. I declared to myself, *He will know us!* He did! When we walked into his room, Mr. Williams rolled over onto his side and faced us. "Hi neighbor!" he greeted Daddy.

"Is that Di with you?" He knew my presence meant a major change for Daddy. I walked over to the bed to give Mr. Williams a hug. Then I excused myself to go to the restroom. There was one in his room, but Daddy and his neighbor needed time alone to say farewell. I stood outside the door in the clean brightly-lit hallway. The walls were sunlight yellow. The floors looked recently waxed, but weren't slippery. The atmosphere was quiet which made it easy for me to hear the two friends talking.

"Is Di here to take you with her?" Mr. Williams asked softly.

"Yeah. I gotta go Preacher. I don't think I can do this by myself anymore," Daddy replied sadly.

"We knew that this day was coming. We talked about it remember?" Mr. Williams questioned.

There was silence. I figured they were both trying to hold back tears as they realized their neighbor days were ending. Daddy broke the silence, "Preacher, you have to come see me in Atlanta soon. You have folks in Alabama, so you can swing by to see us after you visit them." Both men knew that Mr. Williams was bedridden and not likely to go to Alabama to visit family again. But showing the strength and fortitude that they possessed, Mr. Williams responded, "I sure will neighbor!" It was time for me to enter the room and let them off the trying-to-say-goodbye hook.

"BJ, we need to let Mr. Williams get some rest now. Plus we have a few more errands to run before we leave."

I walked to his bedside, gave Mr. Williams a parting hug, and tried to put on a smile as we exited the room. Daddy trailed behind me. By this time, we were battling tears as we walked away from the nursing facility in slow motion.

Mr. Asbury (the Wease)

James Asbury and Daddy were born on August 18th. Mr. Asbury was much younger, but they became good friends as a result of being co-workers and fraternity brothers. Mr. Asbury was born with one regular-sized arm and the other reached from his shoulder to his elbow. That did not stop him from being a stellar basketball player! Every August 18th, Mr. Asbury stopped by with a bottle of whiskey for him and Daddy to celebrate. I never learned how he earned the nickname *Weasel*, but I think it had something to do with his basketball agility. Daddy shortened the moniker to *the Wease*. We could hear Mr. Asbury approaching the house before he actually came in. He spoke loudly and addressed everyone in sight. By the time he finished yelling hello to all the neighbors, Daddy was at the door welcoming him. "Hey Wease, come on in!"

"HEY, HEY, HEY MY MAIN MAN! HAPPY BIRTHDAY!" Mr. Asbury came in the house and screamed hello to us too.

Once Daddy moved to Atlanta, he looked forward to his annual phone call from Mr. Asbury. The Wease never disappointed. Even through the phone, I could hear his voluminous voice from another room! Though they only spoke once a year, Mr. Asbury was definitely one of Daddy's A-list friends. This made it incredibly hard to tell him that the Wease had died. I read about it in the online Gary obituaries. I broke the news to Daddy after dinner. He held his head down in disbelief. Moments later he raised his head. He had a solemn look on his face as if thinking, *Rest in Peace Wease!*

Gracie

Daddy's favorite pooch and personal caregiver developed kidney failure and became ill when she turned 12. Gracie's weight plummeted from 55 pounds to 22 within two months. The veterinarian told us that it was time to euthanize her. I was not ready to do that. She could still walk and eat, although she was just skin, fur, and bones! The doctor said that she could perform a procedure that might help her last another few months. I agreed to it! The vet told us that if she didn't die on her own that her quality-of-life would confirm when it was time to euthanize her.

We watched Gracie perk up for two months before her health started declining again. She could no longer jump on the bed to tell Daddy goodnight, so I lifted her onto it. I also raised her frail body onto the couch to watch TV. Gracie never lost her appetite so I didn't understand her weight loss and weakness. I came home from work one day and she didn't move. She couldn't. That was the confirmation that it was time to say goodbye. Daddy was also saying goodbye to his short-term memory.

Daddy and Sydney went with us to take Gracie to the clinic to be euthanized. After giving her a few treats, Mario carried her outside and placed her in the back of the station wagon. That was always her favorite place to ride. Once we arrived at the clinic, the staff took over. The nurses situated her on a colorful little blanket on a floor in a private room. The staff encouraged us to rub, talk to, and give her kisses as the doctor gave her the lethal injections. We held her paw as she took her last breath. Sydney nuzzled next to her as if encouraging her to get up. We sat for a few minutes before leaving. The ride home was quiet. No one spoke. Sydney didn't even bark. As everyone prepared to go to bed, Daddy asked to see Gracie.

"We took her to the clinic Daddy to put her down?"

"When do we go back to get her?"

"We won't go back Daddy. She's dead."

"She's *DEAD*?" Daddy asked in profound disbelief.

A few tears trickled from his eyes. I turned away so that Daddy couldn't see my tears. I suppose they were a combination of losing Gracie and watching Daddy's memory fade.

Dick

Other than my mom, Dick was Daddy's most painful loss. He was more like a brother than any of Daddy's other close friends. Dick introduced my parents to each other. His real name was Percy. I thought his real name was Richard, since *Dick* is a nickname for Richard. But I learned that he had a brother named Richard, but they called him Fuzzy. I gave up trying to figure that out and just called him Dick like everyone else. His family lived in the same apartment building as my mother's family. No one seems to recall how Daddy and Dick met each other, but he was five years Daddy's junior.

After Daddy regained his memory from his initial stroke nine years prior, the first person he wanted to call in Gary was Dick. Though Daddy's speech was still a bit slurred, he and Dick chatted regularly. They continued to talk throughout Daddy's stay in Atlanta.

One night Dick's wife Irma called to tell us that he had been taken to the hospital after grabbing his side in excruciating pain then passing out. Dick was in the hospital for about three weeks. Daddy told me to send Irma a few dollars to help pay for hospital parking. I must admit that he could be extremely thoughtful with things like helping his friends!

Dick's health improved. Irma phoned me on a Wednesday to tell us that Percy would be home that following Saturday. Daddy was so excited that you would have thought Irma told him that Dick was coming to Atlanta to see him! Irma called me late that Saturday night he was to be discharged. Daddy had gone to bed. Something had to be wrong. First, she had never phoned us late in the evening. Second, I could hear sadness in her voice, as she struggled to tell me that Percy had died. *What! How could that have happened? He was on his way home!* Now I was the one struggling to ask, "What happened?" Irma explained that he was scheduled to come home, when he took a *turn for the worse…*a phrase Black people often used to say that an ill person was dying suddenly instead of getting better. Hearing the quiver in her voice and the sound of sniffling, I knew she was crying. Feeling numb I remember expressing my condolences, thanking her for calling, then slowly placing the phone back in its cradle.

How on earth was I going to tell Daddy that Dick had died? It would break his heart! His best friend for over 50 years! The man who introduced him to my mom…so in a sense was responsible for my existence, was gone! I was sad too, but I had a bigger task at hand than my grieving…informing Daddy!

The next morning started as usual, with Daddy blasting the volume on the TV as he watched the news in his bedroom while dressing. I had a lump in my throat as I prepared to deliver the heartbreaking news. Since his hearing was almost completely gone, I decided that the best thing to do was write the message on a note. I handed him the small piece of paper and stood next to him as he read it. For a few seconds he was still. He didn't respond. *What was going on in his mind?*

"Dick is *dead*?" he finally asked in disbelief.

"Yes Daddy."

"What happened? I thought he was going home?" he uttered slowly.

Putting my arm on his shoulder I replied, "Irma called last night to tell us that something went wrong and he didn't make it out of the hospital."

We both remained frozen for a few minutes. Daddy read the note countless times, folding and unfolding it as if that would magically change its message. I walked in the kitchen to cook breakfast and give Daddy time to digest the news. By the time I finished cooking, Daddy had gone in his bedroom and closed the door.

Had he not been diabetic, I wouldn't have interrupted his solitude. I called him to the kitchen to eat. He was still wiping tears from his eyes. Watching him lose composure was hard for me. The only other time I saw him cry was when Mama died. Then it hit me...this was August and Mama also died in August. The two biggest losses in his life occurred in his birth month. Unbeknownst to me at the time, August would contain the two biggest losses of *my* life as well. Daddy would die the next year, a day after his 94th birthday.

Reflections

- *Farewells and goodbyes are difficult, because we love the people we have to leave.*

- *There are things you can't fix for others, no matter how deeply you love them.*

- *When people you love hurt, you hurt.*

- *We are lucky to love others so deeply that it is painful to say goodbye.*

"There are many reasons why people bid farewell to one another. It may be difficult indeed not to look back. Yet you have to advance, even a step. As long as you advance, new hope will be born. The sun will rise. A new life will unfold for you."
Daisaku Ikeda, President of the Soki Gakki International

Goodbye Daddy

*"The world is truly round and seems to start
and end with those we love."*
Nelson Mandela, former President of South Africa

DADDY WAS IN THE room the day I was born in 1955. I was in the room the day his remains were cremated in 2014. Love filled the room both times. I never doubted Daddy's love for me though he never used the words…except the time he mumbled it to an Emory nurse when he was recovering from his stroke in 2005.

The nurse asked me to step out of the room for a few minutes while she gave Daddy a sponge bath and changed his gown. I stood just a few steps outside of the door, so I could hear her words to him. His speech was slurred, but apparently she understood him. As the nurse performed her tasks, she talked to him.

"Is that your daughter? She is pretty!" the nurse commented. There was a pause and she continued, "Do you love her? You do? How long have you loved her?" Daddy grunted a bit and she translated, "Since the moment you saw her? How sweet!"

Tears gushed in my eyes! I never knew that Daddy loved me the moment he saw me. I had never thought about the exact time that he or Mama first loved me. I know that I loved them until the day *they* died…and will until the day *I* die!

Saying goodbye to Daddy happened over a three-month period. The first signs of change were disinterest in bingo, the casino, and disregard for playing the daily lottery. The latter was so concerning to me, that I called the funeral director to ask what steps to take once he expired.

The final days started with a call from Minnie. I was at work when she phoned with panic in her voice, "Di your dad is complaining of a headache and wants you to take him to the hospital!" Daddy never *wanted* to go to the hospital, so he must have been in severe pain. Her words paralyzed me for a moment as I reflected, *this is where it all started. That damn headache! Then came the heart attack and stroke. He was in his mid-80s then. He slowly rebounded. He is 93 now, I don't think he can pull through this time!* I quickly snapped out of my trance and drove home exceeding all speed limits. When I got home, Daddy was sitting in a chair with his hat on ready to go.

"How you feeling BJ?" I asked cheerfully, trying to mask my nervousness.

"Gotta little headache and I think we need to get it checked out."

"Sure. Give me a minute to grab your medicine, a snack, and let the pups out and I'll be ready."

On our way to the hospital, Daddy asked if we could stop at Wendy's for him to get a hamburger. I smiled and thought, *his head must not be hurting too badly if he wants to eat!* After he gulped down the burger, things got strange!

"I'm glad you came to get me, because Minnie had her boyfriend over. She always has boyfriends over, but I don't tell you about them."

Incredibly confused, I reacted, "What boyfriends?"

He continued talking about a different boyfriend every day! That simply was not true! He eventually moved on to telling me about his deceased friends...as if they were alive. Of all the things he talked about, the headache was not one of them! Something was terribly wrong!

Since I was driving, I couldn't look at his eyes to see if they were glossy or unfocused, but I was thinking that he must have had a mini-stroke. *What else could be the reason for his sudden mental shift?* As if I weren't driving fast enough, I shifted into high speed. Within minutes I whisked into the Emory valet parking garage, jumped out of my seat, then ran around to the passenger's side and pulled Daddy out of the car. He hobbled into the emergency room with his walker. That would be the last time that he moved with a walker. He would be wheelchair-bound thereafter. He never complained about it. Actually, I think he was tired of walking...period.

As we sat in the emergency room waiting to see a doctor, Daddy continued rambling about my childhood, his childhood, and his deceased friends. Only now, he spoke as if they were in the emergency room with us.

"Wease, I am not ready yet. What are you doing here? Dick go get me a sandwich!" he said as if Wease and Dick were sitting next to him.

After a while, I tuned him out and focused on watching TV. I could hear his voice, but stopped trying to make sense of his words. Suddenly he said something that shocked me back to paying attention to what he was saying.

"This may be my last visit to the hospital Miss Jessie."

"What do you mean by that Daddy? We come to the hospital at least once a year. They treat you, then we go home. Why should this be any different?"

"I'm not going home this time," he said with certainty.

It's what he said next that was unforgettable!

"It's okay. I can't live forever! I've had a good life. If it's my time I can't do anything about it and you can't either! You and Mario have done a great job taking care of me. Mario is young and he needs to get on with his life...buy a house, get married, you know! And you... well, you aren't young anymore, but you can still get on with your life!"

I chuckled as I realized that in his signature humorous way, Daddy was saying *thank you* and *goodbye.* In the nearly 10 years he lived with me, my father never verbally thanked me for caring for him, but he showed his appreciation in other ways. Cards, gifts, and money were the major ways he showed affection. After a few minutes I paused and assured him that he would be just fine.

Daddy was admitted to the hospital a few hours later. From that point on his health continued to decline. He lost his ability to walk, developed blisters on his legs, and the insulin no longer controlled his diabetes. I cried when the doctor referred me to the medical social worker to discuss nursing home options. It was looking as if Daddy's prediction was right…he wouldn't be coming back home with me.

We were fortunate to find a nursing home within 10 minutes from my house. I visited Daddy every day. Mario could visit too. We took Sydney once, but Daddy asked us not to bring him again. His health worsened. Several times he had to be transported by ambulance to the Rockdale hospital around the corner from the nursing home for his diabetes management. Nothing worked to improve his condition. The nursing home recommended hospice care after he had been there a month. People who went into hospice died within days. I knew he was dying, but I wasn't ready to say goodbye in a few days.

Immediately after agreeing to hospice care, I had to notify family and friends of the news. I met with the funeral director to plan the cremation. He told me that I could be present all the way until the end if I wanted. At first I wasn't sure, but later decided that I didn't want him to be there alone.

Hospice care wasn't as frightening as I had imagined. Daddy was able to stay in the same nursing home and room. The thing that changed was the level of care the medical staff provided. He reached a point that he no longer spoke. At times, he uttered words to his late sister and mother, but not a word to me. A friend told me that when people are transitioning from life to death, they talk to the people they are going to see…not the ones they are leaving. Another thing transitioning people do is rip their clothes off. That hospital gown with the open back was no match for Daddy. He pulled that thing off like a baby yanks off a bib! The nurse asked me to bring him a t-shirt and exercise pants in hopes that he would keep those on. Nope! No sooner than the nurse dressed and fed him, he was naked! The staff was extremely kind and patient with him. They never seemed irritated by his disrobing behavior and put clothes back on as quickly as he pulled them off.

His third week in hospice was his last. I continued daily visits and took balloons and greeting cards to him to celebrate his 94th birthday. The nursing staff enjoyed the birthday cupcakes I gave them.

At 4:30 the next morning, the phone rang. I jumped up from my bed to answer the phone…anticipating the news. On the other end was a nurse I hadn't met. "Ms. Harvey, I am sorry to tell you that your father just passed. I am so sorry, we loved him. I've called the funeral home and they are sending someone to get him."

"Thank you, I'm on my way." I sent Minnie a text message thinking she would see it when she awakened later.

The drive to the nursing home was dark and silent. I was numb. I was going to see my lifeless father. *How would he look? How would I react?* The night crew of nurses met me at the front door and hugged me. We had never met, but since a nurse called me moments earlier, they knew who I was. One of them asked if I wanted her to accompany me to see Daddy. "No thanks. I can do it," I responded pleasantly.

When I entered his room, I looked at him for what seemed like hours, but was actually only a few minutes. He was motionless and his mouth was open. Standing next to him I spoke softly, thanking him for being my father, loving me, and living with me. I told him that I hope I did a good job caring for him, because I didn't really know what I was doing! Many days I was flying by the seat of my pants hoping that I got things right. I teased, "You often said I was bossing you around like I was *your* parent and reminded me that you were *my* father! I did the best I could and hoped that I was half as good at being a parent to you as you were to me…and for the record, I always knew which one of us was the *real* parent!"

By the time I finished my chat with Daddy, a small man from the funeral home was there to, as he put it, *collect his remains*. I hated that phrase, but I guess that's how they spoke in the funeral business. I was more concerned with who was going to help this tiny man lift my heavy father onto the gurney and roll him to the hearse.

"Is someone here to help you lift my dad?"

"Don't need anyone ma'am. I can do it myself! Let me go to the parking lot and lift the door, so I can roll him in."

"But my dad is much larger than you!" I said sternly.

Minnie walked in at that moment. I wanted her to have a few private seconds with Daddy. I left the room and dashed to the nursing station asking a few of them to go to Daddy's room to help that *little* man slide him onto the gurney! Three of them ran down the hall as the man was coming back into the building. I watched from the window of my car as the nurses helped the man with Daddy, then I drove away.

A few days later I spent my final minutes with Daddy at the funeral home. I was sitting in a small, neat parlor facing a window with floral curtains. Daddy was on the other side of that window. The funeral director asked if others were coming to sit in the room with me. I told him that no one else would be joining me. Like a Broadway play, this scene was literally the final curtain. He said, "Let me know when you are ready and I will pull the curtains so that you can see the other side. You will see your father. His head will be visible and his body will be surrounded by a cardboard box.

Slowly the conveyer belt will move your dad into the furnace. You can leave at any time."

I gave him the thumbs up when I was ready for him to begin. The curtain opened. Daddy looked like he had climbed into a cardboard box and stretched out on his back. His mouth was still open, but he looked peaceful. I watched his body move toward the furnace until it was no longer visible. I smiled and thought, *you were with me when my head popped into the world. I was with you when your head popped out of this world.*

The funeral director closed the curtain. I got up from my seat, turned toward the window, and waved *goodbye* to Daddy!

Reflections

- *Death ends a life, but not a relationship.*

- *Love conquers fears and gives you courage!*

- *When it's over, you are grateful for the experience!*

Reflections Compiled

- *Life has interruptions.*

- *Friends step up during crises. Be thankful for them!*

- *The only preparation you can have for the unknown is determination.*

- *Panic is a natural response to sudden changes!*

- *You have more courage than you think!*

- *Learn what strategies work best with whom you're working.*

- *Sometimes you already have the answers...just think!*

- *Emotional stress can present itself in physical ailments.*

- *Get regular physical checkups.*

- *Search for answers in more than one place.*

- *In the midst of demands or challenges, take a minute to breathe and reflect.*

- *If the person you are caring for is a senior, you must organize their affairs. If they are lucid, do so in a way that empowers them.*

- *You will need their permission to discuss their accounts with creditors, so arrange that as soon as possible. It will involve phone calls or letters. Email communication may also be an option.*

- *Always be gentle when you criticize.*

- *Allow caregivees to retain dignity.*

- *When you love someone, putting their needs first is natural.*

- *You don't owe anyone an explanation for the choices you make...especially as it relates to someone you are responsible for!*

- *Improve on what doesn't work well...don't beat yourself up about it.*

- *Doing something extremely well can be a curse!*

- *Sometimes you lie to spare someone else's feelings.*

- *Be prepared for your loved ones to toss the ball to you, when they don't want to be seen as unkind.*

- *Seeking help with caregiving does not make one weak.*

- *Taking care of self is not selfish.*

- *Therapy may offer support if the counselor understands caregiver stress.*

- *Find something to do that relaxes you. Do it often.*

- *If you don't take care of yourself, you cannot take care of others.*

- *It is important to allow people to keep as much of their enjoyable traditions as possible.*

- *Blending and creating traditions can be fun for everyone and help with adjustment to a new environment.*

- *There are valuable nuggets in the midst of trials. Cherish them!*

- *Farewells and goodbyes are difficult, because we love the people we have to leave.*

- *There are things you can't fix for others, no matter how deeply you love them.*

- *When people you love hurt, you hurt.*

- *We are lucky to love others so deeply that it is painful to say goodbye.*

"There are many reasons why people bid farewell to one another. It may be difficult indeed not to look back. Yet you have to advance, even a step. As long as you advance, new hope will be born. The sun will rise. A new life will unfold for you." Daisaku Ikeda, President of the Soki Gakki International

- *Death ends a life, but not a relationship.*

- *Love conquers fears and gives you courage!*

- *When it's over, you are grateful for the experience!*

Letter From Anita

The sentiment contained in the numerous sympathy cards I received from family and friends is summed up in a handwritten note from my cousin Anita.

Dear Diane,

I hope you rediscovered your Dad. He was always one who wanted to be helpful, to fulfill all the obligations of life, and yet, preserve his spiritual life. He had a hospitality of warmth, friendliness in his words, and a serenity in bearing difficulties while hiding his sufferings. His life was loving his family. I hope you are enjoying sharing his love...he gave you...with others.

Anita

…About Those Promises

My grandmother told me not to make promises that I could not keep. At the time I made a promise, I had every intention of fulfilling it. Some I did. Some I didn't. Unless I could control all the elements in the universe – sickness, aging, death, and everything in between, I learned not to make promises! They were tools that could not be controlled by mere mortals! My best phrase now is, "I'll do my best." That I can handle!

If you made a promise to the person you are now caregiving, you probably made it before they needed care. Now that it is time to cash in on the promise, things may have changed in your life or theirs.

For you who are facing the angst of denying or modifying a promise made years ago, here are a few suggestions that may help you release that feeling. Think about these questions:

- *When was the promise made?*

- *What changed in your life or the other person's life since then?*

- *What modifications can you make to come close to keeping the promise?*

Once you sort out these questions, you can explain to your caregivee the reasons why things have to be readjusted. Perhaps your income changed or you moved from a spacious house to a small apartment. Let's face it, some things changed for the caregivee too, or they wouldn't be in need of help. Discuss those changes and formulate a new plan.

People hold you to promises because they are *afraid*, not insensitive. The person you love is fearful of what will happen to them without your support. Assure them that you will be there for them. The picture may look a bit different than what you imagined years ago, but you will take care of them as best you can...even if that means getting help from others.

Messages to Caregivers and Family and Friends

Dear Caregiver,

You are phenomenal! There may be days when you question that, like I did when I lost Daddy at the VA Hospital – but quickly replace that doubt with the confidence that you are doing the best that you can! And that's pretty darn great!

I wish that I could send you a t-shirt that reads, "Caregiving Gives Me Super Powers!" It does! You have them! Believe it!

The most important thing I want for you is to stay hopeful! My sentiment is expressed in the chorus of Lee Ann Womack's song, I Hope You Dance.

I hope you still feel small when you stand beside the ocean,
Whenever one door closes, I hope one more opens,
Promise me that you'll give faith a fighting chance,
And when you get the choice to sit it out or dance…
I hope you DANCE!

Hugs,

Diane

P.S. If I neglected to mention this, people don't always support you in the ways you want them to, but they help the in ways they can.

Dear Family and Friends of Caregivers,

If you have not experienced caregiving, you may feel lost when trying to support your caregiver, family member, or friend. That's okay!

Send an unexpected token such as a flower, card, or their favorite candy. Oh wait…those are things that I like! Just ask what they want.

Make sure that whatever you do for your friend doesn't create more stress! For example, don't plan a surprise overnight outing for them. That would create pressure to find a caregivee-sitter. Unless you plan on taking along the caregivee…which would defeat the purpose of a getaway.

It's fine if they don't know what they want. Assure them that you will be there…whenever! The song No Man is an Island is befitting.

No man is an island,
No man stands alone,
Each man's joy is joy to me,
Each man's grief is my own.
We need one another,
So I will defend,
Each man as my brother,
Each man as my friend.

Best,

Diane

Resources

The first line of defense when seeking caregiver help is the medical social worker. This person will have the most recent resources for services in your area for your situation.

My caregiving experience was with an elderly parent, so my resources are focused on that population. However, some of these resources might also be able to refer you to the appropriate agencies.

If you are the sole caregiver for the person in your life, it can involve taking control of their finances, making medical and legal decisions, and handling general business on their behalf. This process can involve tons of phone calls, emails, letters, and who knows what else! It can be overwhelming! Suffice to say that organizational skills will be critical to managing their affairs.

The good news is that there are people and agencies that can help you navigate your way through the caregiving maze! Knowing where to find help can soothe the anxiety associated with becoming a caregiver. These services may differ by state, but the list in this section gives you a blueprint for research.

My father moved from another state to live with me. We could not walk into the office of his teacher retirement system to make changes. All changes were made by phone or letter and I had to prove who I was. The acceptable way to do that was to have my father talk to the representative and give them permission to discuss his business matters with me. That was over 15 years ago, so things might be different now. A better plan was contacting a lawyer to get power of attorney over my dad. It was easier to work on his behalf once that was established.

A *power of attorney* is a legal document that allows someone else to act on your behalf. Powers of attorney can be helpful to older people and others who want to choose a trusted person to act when they cannot. This is a must for most caregivers! I kept my power of attorney document in my purse at all times.

If you are taking care of a senior who is collecting Social Security benefits, contacting that office will be necessary to notify them of the address change for the caregivee. You may also have to re-route payments to a new joint account. That takes me to the next resource...banks.

Setting up new or joint accounts at banks can be nerve-racking! The power of attorney document can simplify that process. My father gladly accompanied me to the bank to merge accounts, but this might not be an option for others.

Daddy could not find his birth certificate, which complicated the process of him getting a Georgia Identification Card. He needed the ID card for everything you need a driver's license to do...except drive. For example, when making a bank deposit or withdrawal, he needed to show the teller his ID. Long story short, it took almost six months to get a new birth certificate from his home state, Arkansas. The office of vital records in his home town had burned down decades ago. For them to construct a new birth certificate for him we had to provide his marriage license, my brother's birth certificate, my birth certificate, my mother's death certificate, his Army discharge papers, and any other legal proof we could find with his name on it. We ultimately got a new one, but I wanted to illustrate that things you can't foresee might lead you down a long and winding road! Be patient.

Speaking of patience, when calling agencies be prepared to *wait*. Most agencies will have automated phone systems and you will have to listen to menu options before pressing a number to speak to a representative. Then you have to wait for the representative to finish helping other people before getting to you! Have your questions ready when you call. Also have pen and paper ready to take notes.

Benefits and Services Resources

<u>Elder Care Directory</u>

Eldercaredirectory.org

Elder Care Locator - 800-677-1116

This directory and locator provides essential information for seniors and caregivers. It is available in 50 states and includes:
- *home health guide*
- *residential care options*
- *financial assistance programs*
- *elder law and finance*
- *government programs*
- *Medicaid benefits and pitfalls*

<u>Aging and Disability Resource Centers (ADRC) – **Countrywide**</u>

** Note: The Elder Care Locator will direct you to this page or type Aging and Disability Resource Center in the search bar.*

Georgia Gateway

gateway.ga.gov

Services include:
* *counseling for adults with disabilities, substance abuse, and mental health*
* *assessing eligibility for food stamps, energy assistance, aging services*
* *help for military veterans and families*

Social Security Administration

ssa.gov

The United States Social Security Administration is an independent agency of the U.S. federal government that administers Social Security, a social insurance program consisting of retirement, disability and survivor benefits.

Medicare

medicare.gov
1-800-633-4227

For questions about claims or other personal Medicare information, log into (or create) your secure Medicare account, or call 1-800-MEDICARE (1-800-633-4227). TTY users can call 1-877-486-2048.

Georgia Medicaid
benefits.org
877-423-4746

Medicaid provides health coverage to millions of Americans, including children, pregnant women, parents, seniors and individuals with disabilities. In some states the program covers all low-income adults below a certain income level.

Note: Medicaid is sometimes referred to by state specific names. Regardless of the various names, the programs are still Medicaid and are governed by federal Medicaid law and regulations.

Veteran Administration

va.gov
Veterans Benefit Assistance VBA – 800-827-1000

This website provides a comprehensive list of services available to veterans and families.

Caregiver Health Services

Physical

Taking care of your physical and mental health is vital! Find a medical expert to schedule regular physical checkups. That can include a primary care physician or naturopath. Naturopathic medicine uses natural remedies to help the body heal itself. It embraces many therapies, including herbs, massage, acupuncture, exercise, and nutritional counseling. I combined the two, because my naturopath did not provide mammograms, bone density exams, blood and urine sampling, or other exploratory services. However, once I got a diagnosis, such as low potassium, I went to the naturopath for herbal remedies.

Choose what works best for you, but schedule regular health exams!

Mental Health

Your mental health is equally as important as your physical health. Caregiving is stressful! It is natural to feel overwhelmed. I didn't think anyone understood, so I kept my feelings and stress bottled inside. The result…30-pound weight gain, hypertension, red-eye, and chronic fatigue.

Mental health does not necessary mean seeking a professional therapist. Therapeutic practices can include: support groups, good friends, exercise, journaling, and any other practice that releases emotional pressure.

The medical social worker may also have a list of counselors or services to recommend to the caregiver. If you have insurance through your job, explore the counseling services that they cover. The caregivee may need counseling. If they don't have funds or insurance to cover it check with eldercare services.

Here are two possibilities for those interested in alternative counseling options. Most insurance companies do not cover alternative options.

Life Coach

A life coach is a type of wellness professional who helps people make progress in their lives in order to attain greater fulfillment. Life coaches aid their clients in improving their relationships, careers, and day-to-day lives. These practitioners are usually certified, though some people call themselves *life coaches* with no training. Always ask to see credentials.

Spiritual Director

Spiritual direction is the practice of being with people as they learn to and grow in their personal spirituality. Like life coaches, these practitioners should be certified. Though God-centered, the practice has been helpful to people of diverse religions and beliefs.

Disclaimer:

Listing agencies, services, and practitioners is not an endorsement. Also, some phone numbers may have changed by the publication of this book. A Google search may help find current numbers.

BEST RESOURCE EVER...

SOMEONE WHO HAS GONE THROUGH

WHAT YOU'RE GOING THROUGH!